CONTENTS

BPP LEARNING MEDIA'S AAT MATERIALS

Since July 2010 the AAT's assessments have fallen within the **Qualifications and Credit Framework** and most papers are now assessed by way of an on demand **computer based assessment**. BPP Learning Media has invested heavily to ensure our ground breaking materials are as relevant as possible for this method of assessment. In particular, our **suite of online resources** ensures that you are prepared for online testing by allowing you to practice numerous online tasks that are similar to the tasks you will encounter in the AAT's assessments.

The BPP range of resources comprises:

- **Texts**, covering all the knowledge and understanding needed by students, with numerous illustrations of 'how it works', practical examples and tasks for you to use to consolidate your learning. The majority of tasks within the texts have been written in an interactive style that reflects the style of the online tasks we anticipate the AAT will set. Texts are available in our traditional paper format and, in addition, as ebooks which can be downloaded to your PC or laptop.

- **Question Banks**, including additional learning questions plus the AAT's practice assessment and a number of other full practice assessments. Full answers to all questions and assessments, prepared by BPP Learning Media Ltd, are included. Our question banks are provided free of charge in an online environment containing tasks similar to those you will encounter in the AAT's testing environment. This means you can become familiar with being tested in an online environment prior to completing the real assessment.

- **Passcards**, which are handy pocket-sized revision tools designed to fit in a handbag or briefcase to enable you to revise anywhere at anytime. All major points are covered in the Passcards which have been designed to assist you in consolidating knowledge.

- **Workbooks**, which have been designed to cover the units that are assessed by way of project/case study. The workbooks contain many practical tasks to assist in the learning process and also a sample assessment or project to work through.

- **Lecturers' resources**, providing a further bank of tasks, answers and full practice assessments for classroom use, available separately only to lecturers whose colleges adopt BPP Learning Media material. The practice assessments within the lecturers' resources are available in both paper format and online in e format.

This Text for Accounts Preparation II has been written specifically to ensure comprehensive yet concise coverage of the AAT's new learning outcomes and assessment criteria. It is fully up to date as at June 2012 and reflects both the AAT's unit guide and the practice assessments provided by the AAT.

Each chapter contains:

- Clear, step by step explanation of the topic

- Logical progression and linking from one chapter to the next

- Numerous illustrations of 'how it works'

- Interactive tasks within the text of the chapter itself, with answers at the back of the book. In general, these tasks have been written in the interactive form that students can expect to see in their real assessments

- Test your learning questions of varying complexity, again with answers supplied at the back of the book. In general these test questions have been written in the interactive form that students can expect to see in their real assessments

The emphasis in all tasks and test questions is on the practical application of the skills acquired.

If you have any comments about this book, please e-mail paulsutcliffe@bpp.com or write to Paul Sutcliffe, Senior Publishing Manager, BPP Learning Media Ltd, BPP House, Aldine Place, London W12 8AA.

A NOTE ON TERMINOLOGY

On 1 January 2012, the AAT moved from UK GAAP to IFRS terminology. Although you may be used to UK terminology, you need to now know the equivalent international terminology for your assessments.

The following information is taken from an article on the AAT's website and describes how the terminology changes impact on students studying for each level of the AAT QCF qualification.

What is the impact of IFRS terms on AAT assessments?

The list shown in the table that follows gives the 'translation' between UK GAAP and IFRS.

UK GAAP	IFRS
Final accounts	Financial statements
Trading and profit and loss account	**Income statement or Statement of comprehensive income**
Turnover or Sales	Revenue or Sales Revenue
Sundry income	Other operating income
Interest payable	Finance costs
Sundry expenses	Other operating costs
Operating profit	Profit from operations
Net profit/loss	Profit/Loss for the year/period
Balance sheet	**Statement of financial position**
Fixed assets	Non-current assets
Net book value	Carrying amount
Tangible assets	Property, plant and equipment
Reducing balance depreciation	Diminishing balance depreciation
Depreciation/Depreciation expense(s)	Depreciation charge(s)
Stocks	Inventories
Trade debtors or Debtors	Trade receivables
Prepayments	Other receivables
Debtors and prepayments	Trade and other receivables
Cash at bank and in hand	Cash and cash equivalents
Trade creditors or Creditors	Trade payables

UK GAAP	IFRS
Accruals	Other payables
Creditors and accruals	Trade and other payables
Long-term liabilities	Non-current liabilities
Capital and reserves	Equity (limited companies)
Profit and loss balance	Retained earnings
Minority interest	Non-controlling interest
Cash flow statement	**Statement of cash flows**

This is certainly not a comprehensive list, which would run to several pages, but it does cover the main terms that you will come across in your studies and assessments. However, you won't need to know all of these in the early stages of your studies – some of the terms will not be used until you reach Level 4. For each level of the AAT qualification, the points to bear in mind are as follows:

Level 2 Certificate in Accounting

The IFRS terms do not impact greatly at this level. Make sure you are familiar with 'receivables' (also referred to as 'trade receivables'), 'payables' (also referred to as 'trade payables'), and 'inventories'. The terms sales ledger and purchases ledger – together with their control accounts – will continue to be used. Sometimes the control accounts might be called 'trade receivables control account' and 'trade payables control account'. The other term to be aware of is 'non-current asset' – this may be used in some assessments.

Level 3 Diploma in Accounting

At this level you need to be familiar with the term 'financial statements'. The financial statements comprise an 'income statement' (profit and loss account), and a 'statement of financial position' (balance sheet). In the income statement the term 'revenue' or 'sales revenue' takes the place of 'sales', and 'profit for the year' replaces 'net profit'. Other terms may be used in the statement of financial position – eg 'non-current assets' and 'carrying amount'. However, specialist limited company terms are not required at this level.

Level 4 Diploma in Accounting

At Level 4 a wider range of IFRS terms is needed, and in the case of Financial statements (FNST), are already in use – particularly those relating to limited companies. Note especially that an income statement becomes a 'statement of comprehensive income'.

Note: The information above was taken from an AAT article from the 'assessment news' area of the AAT website (www.aat.org.uk).

ASSESSMENT STRATEGY

Accounts Preparation II (APII) is the second of two financial accounting assessments at Level 3. The AAT recommend that API is studied and taken before APII.

The assessment is normally a two hour computer based assessment.

The APII assessment consists of six tasks, two in Section 1 and four in Section 2.

Section 1 is about incomplete records and will comprise two independent tasks. A variety of techniques for finding missing figures will be required, including a selection from:

- Using the accounting equation
- Using mark-up or margin
- Reconstructing the capital account
- Reconstructing the bank account
- Reconstructing control accounts – purchases, sales, VAT

There may also be short-answer parts testing the knowledge parts of the relevant units

Section 2 is about financial statements for sole traders and partnerships and will comprise four independent tasks. These will include:

- Preparing an income statement from an adjusted trial balance

- Preparing ledger accounts or making calculations to deal with specialised partnership transactions such as admission or retirement of a partner

- Preparing a partnership appropriation account or partners' current accounts

- Preparing a statement of financial position from an adjusted trial balance

- Short answer questions to test the knowledge parts of the relevant units.

Competency

Learners will be required to demonstrate competence in both sections of the assessment. For the purpose of assessment the competency level for AAT assessment is set at 70%. The level descriptor in the table below describes the ability and skills students at this level must successfully demonstrate to achieve competence.

QCF Level descriptor	**Summary**
	Achievement at level 3 reflects the ability to identify and use relevant understanding, methods and skills to complete tasks and address problems that, while well defined, have a measure of complexity. It includes taking responsibility for initiating and completing tasks and procedures as well as exercising autonomy and judgement within limited parameters. It also reflects awareness of different perspectives or approaches within an area of study or work.
	Knowledge and understanding
	▪ Use factual, procedural and theoretical understanding to complete tasks and address problems that, while well defined, may be complex and non-routine
	▪ Interpret and evaluate relevant information and ideas
	▪ Be aware of the nature of the area of study or work
	▪ Have awareness of different perspectives or approaches within the area of study or work
	Application and action
	▪ Address problems that, while well defined, may be complex and non-routine
	▪ Identify, select and use appropriate skills, methods and procedures
	▪ Use appropriate investigation to inform actions
	▪ Review how effective methods and actions have been
	Autonomy and accountability
	▪ Take responsibility for initiating and completing tasks and procedures, including, where relevant, responsibility for supervising or guiding others
	▪ Exercise autonomy and judgement within limited parameters

AAT UNIT GUIDE

Accounts Preparation II (APII)

Introduction

Please read this document in conjunction with the standards for all relevant units.

It is recommended that this unit is taken with, or after Accounts Preparation I.

The QCF units relating to Accounts Preparation I and Accounts Preparation II units overlap. Accounts Preparation I and II have been designed in order to avoid duplication of assessment and match the appropriate parts of the knowledge unit (Principles of accounts preparation) with the corresponding skills.

Successful completion of this AAT unit alone will result in the award of one QCF unit:

- Prepare accounts for partnerships (knowledge and skills)

This unit also covers most of the QCF unit "Prepare final accounts for sole traders" and aspects of the QCF unit "Principles of accounts preparation".

Therefore successful completion of Accounts Preparation II together with Accounts Preparation I will result in the award of four further QCF units:

- Principles of accounts preparation (knowledge)
- Prepare final accounts for sole traders (skills)
- Accounting for fixed assets (skills)
- Extending the trial balance using accounting adjustments (skills)

The purpose of the unit

The unit builds on skills and knowledge acquired in the Level 2 units, Basic Accounting I, Basic Accounting II and Level 3 unit Accounts Preparation I. The unit is concerned with preparing financial statements for sole traders and partnerships, incorporating elements of dealing with incomplete records, and an appropriate understanding of the principles that underpin the preparation of financial statements.

After completion of both Accounts Preparation units, the learner will be ready to start developing skills and knowledge for the Level 4 unit, Financial Statements.

Terminology

Students should be familiar with IFRS terminology. Other terms are used in this document to match titles provided by the QCF. All AAT assessments will use IFRS terminology from 1 January 2012.

Learning objectives

The learner will develop accounting skills in restructuring accounting information from incomplete records and preparing financial statements for a sole trader. The learner will be able to restructure accounts to find missing information and incorporate accruals and prepayments, provisions for depreciation, irrecoverable debts and allowances for doubtful debts.

Learners will need to show understanding of the procedures involved in, and the reasons for, preparing financial statements for sole traders, including an awareness of the accounting systems that a business must put in place in order to produce meaningful information at the end of an accounting period. The learner should also develop an understanding of the environment and principles within which the business operates.

The learner will be introduced to the legal requirements underpinning the preparation of partnership accounts. The learner will be able to prepare final accounts for a partnership showing the division of profits (or losses) after adjusting for interest on capital, interest on drawings and any salaries due to each partner.

Learning outcomes

There are three QCF units involved. Each is divided into component learning outcomes, which in turn comprise a number of assessment criteria.

QCF Unit	Learning Outcome	Assessment Criteria	Covered in Chapter
Prepare final accounts for sole traders (skills)	Prepare accounting records from incomplete information	Calculate accurately the opening and/or closing capital using incomplete information	3
		Calculate accurately the opening and/or closing cash/bank account balance	3
		Prepare sales and purchases ledger control accounts and use these to correctly calculate sales, purchases and bank figures	3
		Calculate accurately account balances using mark ups and margins	3
	Produce accurate final accounts	Prepare an income statement	2
		Prepare a statement of financial position	2
Prepare accounts for partnerships (knowledge and skills)	Have a basic understanding of legislation relating to the formation of a partnership	Describe the key components of a partnership agreement	4
		Identify and describe the key components of partnership accounts	4
	Prepare a profit and loss appropriation account	Prepare the partnership appropriation account	4
		Accurately determine the allocation of profit (or losses) to partners after allowing for interest on capital, interest on drawings and any salary paid to partner(s)	4
		Prepare the current accounts for each partner and calculate the closing balance	4

QCF Unit	Learning Outcome	Assessment Criteria	Covered in Chapter
	Prepare a balance sheet relating to a partnership	Record accurately the closing balances on each partner's capital and current accounts, including drawings	4
		Prepare a statement of financial position for a partnership, in compliance with the partnership agreement	4
Principles of accounts preparation (knowledge)	Understand generally accepted accounting principles and concepts	Explain the accounting characteristics relating to relevance, reliability, comparability, ease of understanding and materiality	1
	Understand the principles of double entry bookkeeping	Explain the meaning of the accounting equation	1, 3
		Describe the meaning of assets, liabilities and capital in an accounting context	1
		Describe the components of a set of financial statements for a sole trader	2
	Understand the need for, and the process involved in, the preparation of final accounts	Identify reasons for closing off accounts and producing a trial balance	2
		Explain the process, and limitations, of preparing a set of financial statements from a trial balance	2
		Describe the methods of constructing accounts from incomplete records	3
		Provide reasons for imbalances resulting from incorrect double entries	2
		Provide reasons for, and give examples of, incomplete records arising from insufficient data and inconsistencies within the data provided	3

Delivery Guidance: Prepare final accounts for sole traders

1 Prepare accounting records from incomplete information

1.1 Calculate accurately the opening and/or closing capital using incomplete information

- Opening and/or closing balances on asset and liability accounts may be given

- T-accounts or calculations may be required

- Application of the accounting equation to find balances may be required.

1.2 Calculate accurately the opening and/or closing cash/bank account balance

- A summary of balances or transactions will be given from which the opening or closing balance must be calculated

- A T-account may be required

- An understanding that a bank statement balance "in credit" is a debit balance in the records of the business and an overdrawn balance is a credit balance in the records of the business

1.3 Prepare sales and purchases ledger control accounts and use these to correctly calculate sales, purchases and bank figures

- Incomplete information will be given. This may include, for example, opening/closing balances, bank receipts and payments, settlement discounts, irrecoverable debts and returns

- Information may be given in the form of day-books; these may include VAT information that must be dealt with correctly

- Some irrelevant data may be supplied; learners will need to identify what is relevant

- Missing figures may include, for example, discounts, returns, irrecoverable debts, cash sales or purchases, closing VAT balance

- T-accounts may be required

1.4 Calculate accurately account balances using mark ups and margins

- Mark-up/gross sales margin will be given as a percentage

- May need to find sales, purchases, opening or closing inventory

- May need to manipulate the "opening inventory + purchases – closing inventory = cost of goods sold" relationship to find missing figures

- Simple calculations to extract net or VAT from a gross figure (ie including VAT) may be required

2   Produce accurate final accounts

2.1 Prepare an income statement

- A balancing adjusted trial balance will be given

- May include balances on accounts that are dealt with in Accounts Preparation I, such as non-current asset disposals, depreciation charges, irrecoverable debts, for example

- May require accounts to be combined before completing pro-forma (for example sales and sales returns) in accordance with organisational policies that will be given

- Be aware that the trial balance may include either cost of goods sold and one closing inventory entry OR two closing inventory entries, for statement of financial position and income statement

- A skeleton pro forma will be given

- Accounts such as discounts received, interest received etc must be classed as 'other income'

2.2 Prepare a statement of financial position

- From a given full balancing adjusted trial balance

- May include balances on accounts that are dealt with in Accounts Preparation I, such as non-current assets, accumulated depreciation, allowance for doubtful debts (should be deducted from trade receivables), accruals, for example

- May include VAT control

- A skeleton pro-forma will be given

Delivery Guidance: Prepare accounts for partnerships

- Number of partners limited to a maximum of three

- Maximum of one change in the partnership during a period

- Where goodwill arises, it will always be introduced and then subsequently eliminated

- Not limited liability partnerships

- Formation of a partnership from a sole trader will not be tested

- Dissolution of a partnership will not be tested

1 Have a basic understanding of legislation relating to the formation of a partnership

1.1 Describe the key components of a partnership agreement

- Learners should be aware of the existence of the Partnership Act 1890 and the circumstances in which the default provisions would be relevant. Recall of the default provisions will not be required.

1.2 Identify and describe the key components of partnership accounts

- Financial statements, comprising income statement, partnership appropriation account and statement of financial position

- Specialised partnership accounts, comprising goodwill, partners' current accounts and partners' capital accounts

2 Prepare a profit and loss appropriation account

2.1 Prepare the partnership appropriation account

2.2 Accurately determine the allocation of profit (or losses)to partners after allowing for interest on capital, interest on drawings and any salary paid to partner(s)

The following points apply to assessment criteria 2.1 and 2.2

- The profit or loss for the period will be given

- All relevant partnership agreement information will be given

- The profit sharing ratio may be expressed as a ratio, fraction or percentage

- A pro forma appropriation account will be given when required

- Alternatives to the appropriation account may be required, for example calculations relating to the appropriations of one partner only

- May involve change in profit share during the period; profit will not necessarily accrue evenly throughout the period

- Interest on capital may need to be calculated accurately according to given information

- Interest on drawings will not need to be calculated

2.3 Prepare the current accounts for each partner and calculate the closing balance

- May include interest on capital, interest on drawings, drawings, salary and share of profit or loss

- Drawings from bank, cash or goods (ignoring VAT)

- Data may be given in the form of a completed appropriation account

- The calculation for interest on capital may be required

- The calculation for interest on drawings will not be required

3 Prepare a balance sheet relating to a partnership

3.1 Record accurately the closing balances on each partner's capital and current accounts, including drawings

- Drawings should be included in the current account

- May include calculations and accounting entries for goodwill introduced and eliminated on admission or retirement of one partner or change in profit sharing ratios of existing partners

- Accounting entries for the introduction and/or elimination of goodwill and/or capital accounts may be required

- Capital injection will be in the form of cash/bank

- Settlement on retirement will be in the form of cash/bank or loan

- Revaluation of non-current assets will not be tested

3.2 Prepare a statement of financial position for a partnership, in compliance with the partnership agreement

- A balancing adjusted trial balance will be given

- The profit or loss for the period will be given. This will need to be transferred to the partners' current accounts in accordance with a given profit sharing ratio expressed as a ratio, fraction or percentage

- An outline pro forma statement of financial position will be given

Delivery Guidance: Principles of accounts preparation

1 Understand generally accepted accounting principles and concepts

1.1 Explain the accounting characteristics relating to relevance, reliability, comparability, ease of understanding and materiality

- Basic awareness of the objectives used when selecting accounting policies and their meaning in simple terms

- Appreciate that materiality sets the threshold for determining relevance

2 Understand the principles of double entry bookkeeping

2.1 Explain the meaning of the accounting equation

- Demonstrate how elements of the equation are affected by simple accounting transactions

2.2 Describe the meaning of assets, liabilities and capital in an accounting context including

- The differences between and meanings of

  - Non-current assets and current assets
  - Tangible and intangible assets
  - Current liabilities and non-current liabilities

- Identification of goodwill as an intangible non-current asset

- Recognising, and understanding why, the balance on the VAT account may be either an asset of a liability

2.3 Describe the components of a set of financial statements for a sole trader

- Income statement and statement of financial position

3 **Understand the need for, and the process involved in, the preparation of final accounts**

3.1 Identify reasons for closing off accounts and producing a trial balance

- To check the accuracy of double entry

- To provide a starting point for the preparation of financial statements

- To clear revenue and expense accounts for the start of the new financial period

3.2 Explain the process, and limitations, of preparing a set of financial statements from a trial balance

- The trial balance does not prove accuracy of records as not all errors affect the trial balance

- Trial balance does not give a profit figure

- Trial balance has to be sorted into income statement and statement of financial position groupings

- Closing inventory has to be recognised in both income statement and statement of financial position, even if the trial balance includes a cost of goods sold account

3.3 Describe the methods of constructing accounts from incomplete records

- Use of control accounts

- Use of mark-up and gross sales margin

- Manipulation of figures in familiar relationships in order to find a missing figure
  - Using the accounting equation
  - Using elements of cost of goods sold

3.4 Provide reasons for imbalances resulting from incorrect double entries

- One-sided entries
- Entry duplicated on one side, nothing on the other
- Unequal entries
- Account balance incorrectly transferred to trial balance

3.5 Provide reasons for, and give examples of, incomplete records arising from insufficient data and inconsistencies within the data provided

- Loss of data as a result of disaster, theft or loss of books or ledgers, including records held on computer

- Inadequate or missing records (eg receivables, purchases)

- Differences between

- – Physical non-current assets, ledger balances, non-current asset register
- – Physical inventory count and inventory records or book figure
- – Cash book and bank statement
- – Purchases ledger accounts and supplier statements

chapter 1:
INTRODUCTION TO FINANCIAL STATEMENTS

chapter coverage 📖

In Accounts Preparation II (APII) we go a step further than the trial balance with which we ended our coverage of Accounts Preparation I (API). For the APII assessment we need to understand the actual financial statements or final accounts that a business will produce from the trial balance, namely the income statement (also known as the profit and loss account or statement of financial performance) and the statement of financial position (also known as the balance sheet). For APII you need to be able to prepare these financial statements for both a sole trader and a partnership.

This chapter also covers some generally accepted accounting principles and concepts that you need to be aware of. The topics that we shall cover are:

✍ The meaning of capital, income and expense, the different categories of asset and liability, and recognising them in the trial balance

✍ The income statement

✍ The statement of financial position

✍ The relationship between the ledger accounts and the income statement and statement of financial position

✍ Accounting standards

✍ Accounting policies

THE MEANING OF THE BALANCES IN A TRIAL BALANCE

In API we saw how to prepare a trial balance from the closing balances on the general ledger accounts. We will now consider what the balances in a trial balance represent. Each balance will be one of the following:

- An asset
- A liability
- Income
- An expense
- Capital

You need to be able to distinguish between each of these types of balance on the basis of what they represent.

Assets are items that the business owns and that it uses in the process of making profits. Assets are split into two main types:

(a) *Non-current assets* are the result of capital expenditure, meaning that the business plans to use the asset over a number of years. They can be of two types:

   (i) *Tangible non-current assets* have a physical form, so they can be checked, counted and valued easily. Examples include **machinery, furniture, fittings, equipment and motor vehicles**. To allocate the asset's cost over the period of time in which it is used, we depreciate tangible non-current assets as we saw in API.

   (ii) *Intangible non-current assets* have no physical form. They cannot be touched or counted, and measuring their value is very difficult. We shall encounter one type of intangible, namely **goodwill**, when we cover partnership accounting in Chapter 4.

(b) *Current assets* are assets which the business expects to use day to day and which change frequently, namely:

- **Inventory**
- **Trade receivables** (amounts owed by credit customers as represented by the sales ledger control account balance): these are treated as current assets since it is expected that the outstanding amounts will be paid within 12 months
- **Prepayments**
- **'Other' receivables** (such as amounts owed by tenants for rent) which are not included in the sales ledger control account
- **Cash at bank, cash in hand** and **petty cash**

Liabilities are amounts that the business owes to other parties. Like assets, liabilities are split into two types:

(a) *Non-current liabilities* are amounts that the business has to repay at a distant time in the future, normally at least after 12 months from now. These are normally **bank loans**, though loans may also come from other parties.

(b) *Current liabilities* are amounts that must be repaid in the short term, ie normally within the next 12 months. They usually comprise:

- **Trade payables** (amounts owed to credit suppliers as recorded in the purchases ledger control account)

- **Bank overdraft**

- **Accruals**

- **'Other' payables** (such as amounts due to a supplier of a new non-current asset which are not included in the purchases ledger control account, or payroll liabilities)

- **VAT** owed to HM Revenue & Customs (HMRC)

Capital is the amount of money that the owner of the business has invested in it at any point in time. It is increased by the business's *income* and reduced by its *expenses*. It is also reduced by the owner's *drawings*. We shall see more about how capital balances are built up and reduced throughout this Text.

HOW IT WORKS

Given below is the trial balance for Hunter Traders, a small business that is not registered for VAT. For each figure we have stated whether it is an asset, liability, income or expense, or capital, with explanation wherever necessary.

	Debits £	Credits £	Category
Non-current assets	10,200		asset
Bank	800		asset
Electricity	240		expense
Loan to the business		2,000	liability
Capital		12,760	(see below)
Distribution costs	80		expense
Discounts received		280	income
Sales		44,000	income
Opening inventory	2,400		(see below)
Receivables	3,800		asset
Payroll expenses (wages and salaries)	10,400		expense
Discounts allowed	440		expense
Payables		2,400	liability
Rent paid	600		expense
Telephone	320		expense
Office costs	160		expense
Drawings	4,000		(see below)
Purchases	28,000		expense
	61,440	61,440	

- Opening inventory – the inventory figure in the trial balance is always the opening inventory, ie the inventory in hand at the beginning of the accounting period, and it is technically an expense. We shall cover this further later in the Text.

- Capital – the capital balance in the trial balance is always the opening capital figure, ie the amount at the beginning of the accounting period. It is a type of liability, being owed by the business to its owner. Capital is increased by profits (the excess of income over expenses) and reduced by losses (the excess of expenses over income) and by drawings (see below)

- Drawings – although these are a debit balance they are neither an expense nor an asset. Drawings are instead a reduction in capital.

4

Task 1

Given below is the trial balance of a small trader N Lawson who is not registered for VAT. In the space next to each balance, indicate with a tick whether the balance is an asset, liability, income, expense or capital.

	Debit £	Credit £	Asset	Liability	Income	Expense	Capital
Rent	480					✓	
Motor van	7,400		✓				
Payables		1,900		✓			
Gas	210					✓	
Discounts received		50			✓		
Distribution costs	310					✓	
Sales		40,800			✓		
Opening inventory	2,100					✓	
Loan		2,000		✓			
Electricity	330					✓	
Capital		7,980					✓
Telephone	640					✓	
Discounts allowed	60					✓	
Purchases	22,600					✓	
Receivables	3,400		✓				
Wages	9,700					✓	
Drawings	4,000					✓	
Office costs	220					✓	
Motor expenses	660		✓			✓	
Bank	620						
	52,730	52,730					

THE FINANCIAL STATEMENTS

The income statement

The INCOME STATEMENT (IS) as it is known under International Accounting Standards is also known as the PROFIT AND LOSS ACCOUNT or STATEMENT OF FINANCIAL PERFORMANCE.

The income statement is a summary of the activity of the business during the year. It sets out that:

INCOME minus EXPENSES equals PROFIT OR LOSS

(a) If the income is greater than the expenses then a PROFIT is made.

(b) If the expenses exceed the income then a LOSS is made.

The income statement is normally laid out in a particular manner. For companies this layout is required by law but for other business it is followed as a matter of best practice.

HOW IT WORKS

The trial balance (TB) for Hunter Traders is reproduced below. Below this is the income statement for Hunter Traders, together with an explanation of the important points. Each item denoted as income or expense from the trial balance is used in the income statement. As you work through each figure in the income statement tick it off on the trial balance and you will see that all of the income and expenses are used up.

There is one difference between this trial balance and the one we saw earlier: we have included the value of the closing inventory of £3,200. This appears as both a debit (asset) and a credit (reduction of an expense). As we proceed we shall see how this works.

Trial balance of Hunter Traders

	Debits £	Credits £	Category
Non-current assets	10,200		asset
Bank	800		asset
Electricity	240		expense
Loan		2,000	liability
Capital		12,760	capital
Distribution costs	80		expense
Discounts received		280	income
Sales		44,000	income
Opening inventory	2,400		expense
Receivables	3,800		asset
Wages	10,400		expense
Discounts allowed	440		expense
Receivables		2,400	liability
Rent	600		expense
Telephone	320		expense
Office costs	160		expense
Drawings	4,000		reduction of capital
Purchases	28,000		expense
Closing inventory	3,200	3,200	asset AND reduction of expense
	64,640	64,640	

Income statement of Hunter Traders

	£	£
Sales revenue		44,000
Less: cost of sales		
Opening inventory	2,400	
Purchases	28,000	
	30,400	
Less: closing inventory	(3,200)	
Cost of sales		(27,200)
Gross profit		16,800
Discounts received		280
		17,080
Less: expenses		
Electricity	240	
Distribution costs	80	
Office costs	160	
Discounts allowed	440	
Wages	10,400	
Rent	600	
Telephone	320	
		(12,240)
Profit for the year		4,840

Explanation

Trading account – you can see that the income statement naturally falls into two sections. One ends in a figure for GROSS PROFIT and the other in a figure for PROFIT FOR THE YEAR (after deducting the expenses from gross profit). The top part of the income statement is technically known as the TRADING ACCOUNT as this is where the sales value of goods is compared to the cost of selling those goods.

Gross profit – the GROSS PROFIT is the profit earned by the trading activities of the business. As you can see it is calculated as the sales value less the cost of those sales.

Cost of sales – the COST OF SALES in a period comprises:

- The cost of purchases made in the period, PLUS

- The cost of the opening inventory that has been used up in the period, LESS

- The cost of the closing inventory that is carried forward at the end of the period to be used up at a later date – hence its description in the final trial balance as a reduction in expense

Expenses – the second part of the income statement consists of a list of all of the expenses of the business. These are deducted from gross profit to arrive at a figure for profit for the year.

Discounts – discounts allowed to customers are an expense of the business and are therefore included in the list of expenses. Discounts received however are similar to income as they are a benefit to the business. In this income statement they have been shown as miscellaneous income just beneath the gross profit figure, and this is how they will be shown in the exam. It is also possible to show them as a negative expense in the list of expenses (with brackets around as they are to be deducted from the expenses).

Profit for the year – the PROFIT FOR THE YEAR is the final profit of the business after all of the expenses have been deducted.

Task 2

A business has made sales of £136,700 and its purchases totalled £97,500. The opening inventory was £11,300 and the closing inventory was £10,600. What is the business's gross profit?

£ ▨▨▨▨▨▨▨▨

Statement of financial position

Whereas the income statement (IS) is a summary of the income and expense transactions of the business **during the accounting period,** the STATEMENT OF FINANCIAL POSITION (SFP) as it is known under International Accounting Standards is a 'snap-shot' of the business **on the final day of the accounting period.** The SFP is also known as the BALANCE SHEET.

The statement of financial position is a list of all the assets, liabilities and capital balances of the business. It is also an expression of the accounting equation. Remember that the accounting equation is:

ASSETS minus LIABILITIES equals CAPITAL

The statement of financial position is a vertical form of the accounting equation. It lists and totals the assets of the business and deducts the liabilities to arrive at NET ASSETS. This total is then shown to be equal to the capital of the business.

HOW IT WORKS

We will continue with the example of Hunter Traders. In the trial balance that we ticked off when producing the income statement there are now a number of un-ticked items. These will all appear in the statement of financial position.

Again companies have to produce a statement of financial position in a particular format which you do not need to be aware of but most other businesses also produce statements of financial position in a similar manner and this is illustrated below for Hunter Traders.

Statement of financial position of Hunter Traders

	£	£	£
Non-current assets			10,200
Current assets			
Inventory – the asset in the TB	3,200		
Receivables	3,800		
Bank	800		
		7,800	
Current liabilities			
Payables		(2,400)	
Net current assets			5,400
			15,600
Non-current liabilities			
Loan			(2,000)
			13,600

Financed by:

	£
Owner's capital	
Opening capital	12,760
Add: profit for the year from the income statement	4,840
	17,600
Less: drawings	(4,000)
	13,600

Explanation

Accounting equation – the statement of financial position falls naturally into two parts which are the two sides of the accounting equation – 'assets minus liabilities' and 'capital'. (Under International Accounting Standards it can be presented in a different format, with assets in the top half and capital plus liabilities in the bottom half.)

Non-current assets – non-current assets are always shown as the first assets on the income statement being the major long-term assets of the business.

Current assets – the current assets of a business are the other, shorter term assets. These are listed in a particular order starting with the asset that would take longest to realise as cash (the 'least liquid' asset), namely inventory . This is then followed by receivables, prepayments if there are any, and then finally by the most liquid assets: the bank account and cash in hand or petty cash.

Current liabilities – the current liabilities of a business are the short term payables and accruals if there are any. If the business has a credit balance on its cash book at the period end, ie an overdraft, then this is also shown as a current liability. Usually businesses owe VAT to HMRC at the accounting year end, so the balance on the VAT control account would appear as a current liability (a credit).

Net current assets – the NET CURRENT ASSETS figure is a sub-total of the current assets less the current liabilities. The net current asset total is then added to the non-current asset total.

Non-current liabilities – these are liabilities that are due to be paid after more than one year. In this case we have assumed that the loan is a long term loan, ie it is repayable after more than one year. The total for long term liabilities is deducted from the total of non-current assets and net current assets to give the STATEMENT OF FINANCIAL POSITION TOTAL. In terms of the accounting equation this is the total of the assets minus liabilities, that is the business's net assets.

Capital – the capital section of the statement of financial position shows the amounts that are owed by the business to its owner. This consists of:

- The amount of OPENING CAPITAL at the start of the accounting period, PLUS

- The profit that the business has earned, being the figure of £4,840 that is the profit for the year taken from the income statement, LESS

- The DRAWINGS that the owner has taken out of the business during the accounting period.

The total of the capital section is again the statement of financial position total figure, since:

CAPITAL = ASSETS – LIABILITIES

Drawings – these are deducted from capital in the statement of financial position. They are NOT included as expenses in the income statement – they are a reduction of the amount that is owed to the owner by the business.

Task 3

Given below is the trial balance of N Lawson. In the space next to each balance you should indicate with a tick whether the balance would appear in the income statement or in the statement of financial position.

	Debit £	Credit £	Income statement	Statement of Financial position
Rent	480			
Motor van	7,400			
Payables		1,900		
Gas	210			
Discounts received		50		
Distribution costs	310			
Sales		40,800		
Opening inventory	2,100			
Loan		2,000		
Electricity	330			
Capital		7,980		
Telephone	640			
Discounts allowed	60			
Purchases	22,600			
Receivables	3,400			
Wages	9,700			
Drawings	4,000			
Office costs	220			
Motor expenses	660			
Bank	620			
	52,730	52,730		

Ledger accounts and the income statement and statement of financial position

Before we leave the subject of the financial statements we must consider how the income statement and the statement of financial position are prepared from the general ledger accounts.

There is a distinct difference between the income statement ledger accounts and the statement of financial position ledger accounts.

Income statement

The income statement is effectively a large ledger account in its own right. This means that each of the balances on income and expense accounts are cleared to the INCOME STATEMENT LEDGER ACCOUNT at the end of the accounting period. The effect of this is that there is no opening balance on the income and expense ledger accounts at the start of the following accounting period.

Statement of financial position

In contrast the statement of financial position is a list of all of the balances on the asset and liability accounts. These assets and liabilities will still exist at the start of the next accounting period and therefore the balances on these accounts are simply listed in the statement of financial position and then remain in the ledger account as the opening balance at the start of the next accounting period, ie the next day.

HOW IT WORKS

Given below are the balances on the sales account and sales ledger control account for a business at the end of its accounting period.

Sales account

Date	Details	£	Date	Details	£
			31 Dec	Balance b/d	115,000

Sales ledger control account

Date	Details	£	Date	Details	£
31 Dec	Balance b/d	24,000			

Since the sales account is an income account, it is cleared out to the income statement leaving no opening balance on the account at the start of January.

Sales account

Date	Details	£	Date	Details	£
31 Dec	Income statement	115,000	31 Dec	Balance b/d	115,000

In contrast the balance on the sales ledger control account, being an asset, is simply listed in the statement of financial position and then remains in the ledger account as the opening balance.

Sales ledger control account

Date	Details	£	Date	Details	£
31 Dec	Balance b/d	24,000	31 Dec	Balance c/d	24,000
		24,000			24,000
1 Jan	Balance b/d	24,000			

ACCOUNTING STANDARDS

The accounting profession regulates the preparation of financial statements, or final accounts, by means of ACCOUNTING STANDARDS. Their aims are to ensure that financial statements have certain desirable characteristics, as we shall see shortly.

The only accounting standards that are included at Level 3 are covered in Accounts Preparation I (API), namely:

IAS 2   Inventories

IAS 16   Property, plant and equipment

Accounting practice in the UK and elsewhere is very much influenced by International Accounting Standards (IASs), which usually cover the same areas as UK standards but in slightly different ways. The equivalent UK standards that are covered in API are:

SSAP 9   Stock and long-term contracts

FRS 15   Tangible fixed assets

ACCOUNTING POLICIES

Financial statements for a business will be prepared according to:

- Accounting standards

- A number of well-known and well-understood accounting concepts, and

- The business's own accounting policies.

There are many choices to be made when presenting information in financial statements. For example some businesses may treat particular costs as part of cost of sales whereas others may treat the same costs as expenses.

*The choices that a business makes when preparing financial statements are known as its ACCOUNTING POLICIES. The choice of accounting policies that a business makes is fundamental to the picture shown by the financial statements.

Objectives in selecting accounting policies

There are four objectives against which a business should judge the appropriateness of accounting policies to its own particular circumstances. These objectives are:

- RELEVANCE
- RELIABILITY
- COMPARABILITY
- EASE OF UNDERSTANDING

In addition, the business needs to take the concept of materiality into account.

Relevance

Financial information is said to be **relevant** if:

- It has the ability to influence the economic decisions of the users of that information, and

- It is provided in time to influence those decisions.

Where a business faces a choice of accounting policies it should choose the one that is most relevant in the context of the financial statements as a whole.

Reliability

Accounting is not an exact science. As you have seen in your studies for API, many estimates and management decisions have to be made when determining the figures that will appear in the financial statements, for instance for depreciation and inventory. It may never be possible to judge whether such estimates are correct or not, but the accounting policies chosen by a business must ensure that the figures that appear in the financial statements are **reliable**.

There are four aspects to providing reliable information in the financial statements:

- The figures should represent the substance of the transactions or events

- The figures should be free from bias, ie they should be neutral

- The figures should be free from material errors
- A degree of caution must be applied in making judgements where there is uncertainty (known as PRUDENCE).

Comparability

Information in financial statements is used by many different people and businesses, from employees and owners to payables, HMRC and the bank. The information provided in the financial statements is much more useful to these users if it is comparable over time and also with similar information about other businesses. The selection of appropriate accounting policies and their consistent use should provide such comparability.

Ease of understanding

If the financial statements of a business are to be useful then they must be understandable. Accounting policies should be chosen to ensure ease of understanding for users of the financial statements who have:

- A reasonable knowledge of business and economic activities and accounting and
- A willingness to study the information diligently.

Materiality

The MATERIALITY CONCEPT concerns the accounting treatment of "small" or non-material items in the financial statements. What it means in practical terms is that although there are certain rules which underlie the preparation of financial statements, these rules do not need to apply to non-material items.

For example we have seen that assets that are for long-term use in the business should be shown as non-current assets in the statement of financial position. However small items such as calculators and staplers for use in the office need not be treated as non-current assets if it is decided that they are not material – instead their cost is simply an expense in the income statement. Similarly office stationery is charged in full as an expense in the income statement even if there is stock of stationery left at the end of the year. Since these amounts are usually immaterial, no adjustment is needed.

What is a material amount? The answer to this will depend upon the size of the business itself. In some large businesses the materiality level may be set at something like £5,000. However in a small business it would be much lower, with balances of perhaps £100 or even less being considered immaterial.

If an item in the accounts of a business is too small to be material then it cannot be useful to the users of the financial statements and therefore has no **relevance** (see above). So immaterial items are not considered important in the preparation of financial statements.

Task 4

Enter the numbers of the following International Accounting Standards:

Inventories: IAS ☐

Property, plant and equipment: IAS ☐

CHAPTER OVERVIEW

- Debit balances in the trial balance will either be expenses, assets or drawings

- Credit balances in the trial balance will either be income, liabilities or capital

- The opening inventory figure in the trial balance is an expense

- The closing inventory figures in the trial balance are

  - An asset and

  - A reduction in an expense

- The income statement is a historical summary of the activities of the business during the accounting period. It shows the income of the business minus the expenses, split into

  - The trading account, which deducts cost of goods sold from sales revenue to arrive at gross profit

  - The remainder of the income statement, which deducts expenses from gross profit to arrive at profit for the year

- Discounts allowed are expenses deducted to arrive at profit for the year. Discounts received should be shown as income just below gross profit

- The statement of financial position is a 'snapshot' of the business on the last day of the accounting period listing all of the assets, liabilities and capital of the business

- The statement of financial position is a vertical form of the accounting equation showing that the assets minus the liabilities (net assets) equal the capital balance

- Assets are listed in a particular order starting with non-current assets and followed by current assets. The current assets are listed in a particular order starting with the least liquid, inventory, and working down to the most liquid, bank and cash balances

- Current liabilities are the payables of the business that are due to be paid in less than 12 months' time – current liabilities are deducted from the total of the current assets to give a figure known as net current assets

- Non-current liabilities payable after more than 12 months are deducted from the total of the non-current assets and net current assets, to give the final statement of financial position total (net assets)

- Capital is made up of the opening balance of capital plus the profit for the year from the income statement less the owner's drawings. This calculation should give the statement of financial position total, that is capital = net assets (assets less liabilities)

CHAPTER OVERVIEW CONT'D

- Income and expense ledger accounts are cleared to the income statement ledger account at the end of the accounting period leaving no remaining balance on these accounts

- The statement of financial position ledger accounts – asset, liability and capital account balances – on the last day of the accounting period remain in the ledger accounts to become the opening balances at the start of the next accounting period

- Appropriate accounting policies should be chosen by considering and balancing four objectives – relevance (including materiality), reliability, comparability and ease of understanding

- The materiality concept allows immaterial items to be treated in a manner which would not be appropriate for material items – the level of materiality will depend upon the size of the business

Keywords

Income statement – one of the main financial statements showing the income of the business less the expenses of the business for the last accounting period

Gross profit – the profit earned by the business from its trading activities – shown in the trading account

Profit for the year – the final profit of the business after all expenses have been deducted

Statement of financial position – a list of all of the assets, liabilities and capital of the business on the last day of the accounting period

Current assets – the short term assets of the business – inventory, receivables and cash and bank balances

Current liabilities – liabilities that are due to be paid within one year of the statement of financial position date

Net assets – total assets less total liabilities

Net current assets – the total of the current assets minus the current liabilities

Non-current liabilities – liabilities that are due to be paid more than a year after the statement of financial position date

Accounting policies – the accounting methods chosen by a business to produce its financial statements

Relevance – ability to influence the economic decisions of users, affected by materiality among other things

Reliability – accurate and unbiased recording of the substance of a transaction

Comparability – meaningful comparison is possible of financial information over time and between one business and another

Ease of understanding – how easy it is for users with reasonable financial knowledge to understand the financial statements

Prudence – a degree of caution must be applied in making judgements where there is uncertainty

Materiality – the rules of accounting do not need to be applied to immaterial ('small') items

TEST YOUR LEARNING

Test 1

Given below is the trial balance for a small business that is not registered for VAT. You are required to state, in the space next to each balance, whether it is an asset, liability, income, expense or capital, and whether the balance would appear in the income statement (IS) or the statement of financial position (SFP).

	Debit £	Credit £	Type of balance	IS or SFP
Sales		41,200		
Loan		1,500		
Wages	7,000			
Non-current assets	7,100			
Opening inventory	1,800			
Receivables	3,400			
Discounts received		40		
Postage	100			
Bank	300			
Capital		9,530		
Rent	500			
Purchases	30,100			
Payables		2,500		
Discounts allowed	70			
Drawings	3,000			
Electricity	800			
Telephone	600			
	54,770	54,770		

Test 2

Complete the following sentences:

(a) The gross profit of a business is the profit from

(b) The total of the current assets minus the current liabilities is known as

(c) Current liabilities are

(d) Long-term liabilities are

Test 3

The fact that staplers for the office have been charged as an expense to the income statement is an example of which accounting concept?

Test 4

Identify and explain each of the four objectives which should be considered in selecting accounting policies.

chapter 2
FINANCIAL STATEMENTS FOR A SOLE TRADER

___ **chapter coverage** 📖 ___

In Accounts Preparation I we saw how to perform double entry bookkeeping, how to prepare a simple trial balance and how to account for adjustments such as depreciation, accruals and prepayments, irrecoverable debts and doubtful debts, and closing inventory. We also looked at various reconciliations that are prepared at the end of an accounting period and how to deal with suspense accounts and errors. We now bring all of this together in preparing a set of financial statements for a business from a trial balance.

We start this chapter with one element of the accounts for a small business with a single owner – a sole trader – which we have not yet covered in detail, namely the interrelationships between capital, profit and drawings. Then we will work through a full example showing how to go from the year end balances for a sole trader to the financial statements via an initial trial balance and various accounting adjustments. The topics we cover are:

✍ The records and accounts of a sole trader

✍ Preparing the initial trial balance

✍ Setting up and clearing a suspense account

✍ Processing year end adjustments and preparing an amended trial balance

✍ Preparing the income statement and statement of financial position

THE RECORDS AND ACCOUNTS OF A SOLE TRADER

A business which has only one individual as its owner and which does not operate as a company is a SOLE TRADER. There is no legal distinction between the business and the individual but for accounting purposes we treat them as separate entities. The business's accounts reflect only the business's transactions (sales, purchases, other expenses), not the individual's transactions (their mortgage or food bills, for example). They do however reflect the individual's transactions with the business, such as when they take out cash for their personal benefit (known as DRAWINGS).

A sole trader's financial statements consist of an income statement which shows the income and expenses of the accounting period and a statement of financial position which lists the assets and liabilities of the business on the last day of the accounting period.

The bottom section of the statement of financial position sets out how the business is financed and shows:

- The amount of capital the sole trader has paid into the business

- The profit that has been earned over time, including the current accounting year and

- The drawings that the sole trader has taken out of the business in the year.

This section in effect shows the amount that is owed by the business back to the owner or, in other words, the amount that the owner has invested in the business.

HOW IT WORKS

On 1 April 20X8 Dawn Fisher set up her T shirt design business by paying £60,000 of capital into a business bank account. During the year ending 31 March 20X9 Dawn's business made a profit for the year of £11,570 and Dawn withdrew £10,715 from the business for living expenses.

Dawn's capital ledger account could be drawn up as follows

Capital

		£			£
31 Mar	Drawings	10,715	1 Apr	Bank	60,000
31 Mar	Balance c/d	60,855	31 Mar	Profit	11,570
		71,570			71,570
			1 Apr	Balance b/d	60,855

In Dawn's statement of financial position the bottom part – the financing section – would be shown as:

	£
Capital at 1 April 20X8	60,000
Profit for the year	11,570
	71,570
Less: drawings for the year	(10,715)
Capital at 31 March 20X9	60,855

All of the profit of the business is owed back to Dawn by the business and she can withdraw as much or as little in drawings as she considers appropriate.

Task 1

A sole trader has opening capital of £23,400, earns a profit for the year of £14,500 and takes out £12,200 of drawings.

What is the capital of the business at the end of the year?

£ ▢

Drawings

DRAWINGS are cash and goods that the owner of a business takes out of the business for his/her own use. Drawings in cash are accounted for as follows:

DEBIT   Drawings account

CREDIT   Bank account

In some cases however the owner may take goods out of the business. For example the owner of a food shop may take food off the shelves for her own meals.

The most common double entry for this is:

DEBIT   Drawings account

CREDIT   Purchases account

with the cost to the business of these goods.

An alternative method is to:

DEBIT   Drawings account

CREDIT   Sales account

with the selling price of the goods.

Either method is acceptable although the 'Purchases account' method is the most common.

Task 2

The owner of a business takes goods which had cost the business £400 for his own use.

What is the double entry for this?

DEBIT	

CREDIT	

PREPARING FINANCIAL STATEMENTS

We shall now work through a comprehensive example which will take you from ledger account balances through to an income statement and statement of financial position for a sole trader.

HOW IT WORKS

Given below are the brought down balances on the ledger accounts at the end of the day on 31 March 20X9 for John Thompson, a sole trader whose year end is 31 March.

Building at cost

		£		£
31 Mar	Balance b/d	100,000		

Furniture and fittings at cost

		£		£
31 Mar	Balance b/d	4,800		

Motor vehicles at cost

		£		£
31 Mar	Balance b/d	32,700		

Computer at cost

		£		£
31 Mar	Balance b/d	2,850		

Accumulated depreciation – building

	£			£
		31 Mar	Balance b/d	4,000

Accumulated depreciation – furniture and fittings

	£			£
		31 Mar	Balance b/d	1,920

Accumulated depreciation – motor vehicles

	£			£
		31 Mar	Balance b/d	7,850

Accumulated depreciation – computer

	£			£
		31 Mar	Balance b/d	950

Inventory

		£		£
31 Mar	Balance b/d	4,400		

Bank

		£		£
31 Mar	Balance b/d	3,960		

Petty cash

		£		£
31 Mar	Balance b/d	100		

Sales ledger control

		£		£
31 Mar	Balance b/d	15,240		

Purchases ledger control

	£			£
		31 Mar	Balance b/d	5,010

Capital

	£			£
		31 Mar	Balance b/d	130,000

Sales

	£			£
		31 Mar	Balance b/d	155,020

Sales returns

		£			£
31 Mar	Balance b/d	2,100			

Purchases

		£			£
31 Mar	Balance b/d	80,200			

Purchases returns

		£			£
			31 Mar	Balance b/d	1,400

Bank charges

		£			£
31 Mar	Balance b/d	200			

Discounts allowed

		£			£
31 Mar	Balance b/d	890			

Discounts received

		£			£
			31 Mar	Balance b/d	1,260

Wages

		£			£
31 Mar	Balance b/d	32,780			

Rates

		£			£
31 Mar	Balance b/d	5,500			

Telephone

		£			£
31 Mar	Balance b/d	1,140			

Electricity

		£			£
31 Mar	Balance b/d	1,480			

Insurance

		£			£
31 Mar	Balance b/d	1,500			

Motor expenses

		£		£
31 Mar	Balance b/d	1,580		

Office expenses

		£		£
31 Mar	Balance b/d	960		

Allowance for doubtful debts

	£			£
		31 Mar	Balance b/d	220

VAT control

	£			£
		31 Mar	Balance b/d	820

Drawings

		£		£
31 Mar	Balance b/d	15,800		

Preparing the initial trial balance

Step 1   **The first stage is to transfer all of the closing balances on the ledger accounts to the trial balance, add it up and check that it balances.**

This process is completed for two reasons:

- To check that the double entry has been performed accurately. If the trial balance does not balance then there has been at least one error of double entry, such as one-sided entries, an entry duplicated on one side with nothing on the other, unequal entries or an account balance transferred incorrectly to the trial balance, or omitted entirely

- To provide a starting point for the preparation of financial statements

However, preparing a set of financial statements from a trial balance has limitations:

- The trial balance does not prove accuracy of records as some errors do not affect whether the trial balance actually balances – namely errors of principle, errors of original entry, errors of omission and commission and errors where entries are reversed

- The trial balance does not give a profit figure. This needs to be calculated by deducting all expenses from all forms of income

- The trial balance has to be sorted into income statement and statement of financial position groupings

If the trial balance does not balance, first check your additions and if this doesn't clear it, then open up a suspense account to make the debits and credits equal.

Draft trial balance as at 31 March 20X9

	Debit £	Credit £
Buildings at cost	100,000	
Furniture and fittings at cost	4,800	
Motor vehicles at cost	32,700	
Computer at cost	2,850	
Accumulated depreciation – buildings		4,000
Accumulated depreciation – furniture and fittings		1,920
Accumulated depreciation – motor vehicles		7,850
Accumulated depreciation – computer		950
Inventory	4,400	
Bank	3,960	
Petty cash	100	
Sales ledger control	15,240	
Purchases ledger control		5,010
Capital		130,000
Sales		155,020
Sales returns	2,100	
Purchases	80,200	
Purchases returns		1,400
Bank charges	200	
Discounts allowed	890	
Discounts received		1,260
Wages	32,780	
Rates	5,500	
Telephone	1,140	
Electricity	1,480	
Insurance	1,500	
Motor expenses	1,580	
Office expenses	960	
Allowance for doubtful debts		220
VAT		820
Drawings	15,800	
Suspense	270	
	308,450	308,450

Suspense account

In this case the credit total was £270 larger than the debit total and so a suspense account with a £270 debit balance was opened for the difference. The suspense account must of course be cleared and the errors that were discovered are given below:

(a) The purchases returns account was overcast by £100

(b) £200 of office expenses has been charged to the motor expenses account

(c) Discounts allowed of £170 had been correctly accounted for in the sales ledger control account but omitted from the discounts allowed account

Step 2 **We must now prepare journal entries to correct these errors and to clear the suspense account.**

Journal entries

(a) As purchase returns are a credit balance, if the account has been overstated then the purchases returns account must be debited and the suspense account credited.

	Debit	Credit
	£	£
Purchases returns	100	
Suspense		100

(b) As the motor expenses account has been wrongly debited with office expenses the motor expenses account must be credited and office expenses debited.

	Debit	Credit
	£	£
Office expenses	200	
Motor expenses		200

(c) The correct double entry for discounts allowed is a debit to the discounts allowed account and a credit to sales ledger control. The credit has been done but the debit is missing. Therefore debit discounts allowed and credit the suspense account.

	Debit	Credit
	£	£
Discounts allowed	170	
Suspense		170

Year end adjustments

You are also given information about the following year end adjustments that must be made:

(a) Depreciation is to be provided for the year on the following basis:

- Building – 2% on cost
- Furniture and fittings – 20% on cost
- Motor vehicles – 30% on the reducing, or diminishing balance
- Computer – 33 $\frac{1}{3}$% on cost

(b) Rates of £500 are to be accrued

(c) The insurance account includes an amount of £300 prepaid

(d) An irrecoverable debt of £240 is to be written off

(e) An allowance for doubtful debts of £300 is to be made

Step 3 **We must now prepare the journal entries that will complete these adjustments and close off the accounts for the period.**

Journal entries

(a) The accumulated depreciation accounts in the trial balance are the balances at the beginning of the year as the annual depreciation charge has yet to be accounted for. In each case the double entry is to debit a depreciation expense account and to credit the relevant provision account.

	Debit £	Credit £
Depreciation expense – building (100,000 × 2%)	2,000	
Accumulated depreciation – building		2,000
Depreciation expense – furniture and fittings (4,800 × 20%)	960	
Accumulated depreciation – furniture and fittings		960
Depreciation expense – motor vehicles ((32,700 – 7,850) × 30%)	7,455	
Accumulated depreciation – motor vehicles		7,455
Depreciation expense – computer (2,850 × 33 $\frac{1}{3}$%)	950	
Accumulated depreciation – computer		950

(b) Rates of £500 are to be accrued.

	Debit £	Credit £
Rates	500	
Accruals		500

(c)   Insurance has been prepaid by £300.

	Debit £	Credit £
Prepayments	300	
Insurance		300

(d)   An irrecoverable debt of £240 is to be written off.

	Debit £	Credit £
Irrecoverable debts expense	240	
Sales ledger control		240

(e)   Allowance for doubtful debts of £300 is required.

	£
Allowance required	300
Current level of allowance	220
Increase in allowance	80

	Debit £	Credit £
Allowance for doubtful debts adjustment	80	
Allowance for doubtful debts		80

Closing inventory

The closing inventory has been counted and valued at £5,200.

The inventory figure in the draft trial balance is the opening inventory which will eventually be debited to the income statement as part of cost of sales. The closing inventory must now be entered into the accounts with a journal entry.

	Debit £	Credit £
Inventory – statement of financial position	5,200	
Inventory – income statement		5,200

Updating ledger accounts

All of the journal entries have now been made for the correction of errors, adjustments and closing inventory.

Step 4   **The journals must now be entered into the ledger accounts and the ledger accounts balanced to give their amended closing balances.**

This means a number of new ledger accounts have to be opened.

Errors

(a)

Purchases returns

		£			£
31 March	Journal	100	31 March	Balance b/d	1,400
31 March	Balance c/d	1,300			
		1,400			1,400
			31 March	Balance b/d	1,300

Suspense account

		£			£
31 March	Balance b/d	270	31 March	Journal	100

(b)

Office expenses

		£			£
31 March	Balance b/d	960			
31 March	Journal	200	31 March	Balance c/d	1,160
		1,160			1,160
31 March	Balance b/d	1,160			

Motor expenses

		£			£
31 March	Balance b/d	1,580	31 March	Journal	200
			31 March	Balance c/d	1,380
		1,580			1,580
31 March	Balance b/d	1,380			

(c)

Discounts allowed

		£			£
31 March	Balance b/d	890			
31 March	Journal	170	31 March	Balance c/d	1,060
		1,060			1,060
31 March	Balance b/d	1,060			

Suspense account

		£			£
31 March	Balance b/d	270	31 March	Journal	100
			31 March	Journal	170
		270			270

Year end adjustments

(a) Depreciation charges for the year

Depreciation expense – building

31 March	Journal	£ 2,000			£

Accumulated depreciation – building

		£	31 March	Balance b/d	£ 4,000
31 March	Balance c/d	6,000	31 March	Journal	2,000
		6,000			6,000
			31 March	Balance b/d	6,000

Depreciation expense – furniture and fittings

31 March	Journal	£ 960			£

Accumulated depreciation – furniture and fittings

		£	31 March	Balance b/d	£ 1,920
31 March	Balance c/d	2,880	31 March	Journal	960
		2,880			2,880
			31 March	Balance b/d	2,880

Depreciation expense – motor vehicles

31 March	Journal	£ 7,455			£

Accumulated depreciation – motor vehicles

		£	31 March	Balance b/d	£ 7,850
31 March	Balance c/d	15,305	31 March	Journal	7,455
		15,305			15,305
			31 March	Balance b/d	15,305

Depreciation expense – computer

31 March	Journal	£ 950			£

Accumulated depreciation – computer

		£			£
			31 March	Balance b/d	950
31 March	Balance c/d	1,900	31 March	Journal	950
		1,900			1,900
			31 March	Balance b/d	1,900

(b) Rates accrual

Rates

		£			£
31 March	Balance b/d	5,500			
31 March	Journal	500	31 March	Balance c/d	6,000
		6,000			6,000
31 March	Balance b/d	6,000			

Accruals

		£			£
			31 March	Journal	500

(c) Insurance prepaid

Insurance

		£			£
31 March	Balance b/d	1,500	31 March	Journal	300
			31 March	Balance c/d	1,200
		1,500			1,500
31 March	Balance b/d	1,200			

Prepayments

		£		£
31 March	Journal	300		

(d) Irrecoverable debt write off

Irrecoverable debts expense

		£		£
31 March	Journal	240		

Sales ledger control

		£			£
31 March	Balance b/d	15,240	31 March	Journal	240
			31 March	Balance c/d	15,000
		15,240			15,240
31 March	Balance b/d	15,000			

(e)   Allowance for doubtful debts

Allowance for doubtful debts adjustment

		£			£
31 March	Journal	80			

Allowance for doubtful debts

		£			£
			31 March	Balance b/d	220
31 March	Balance c/d	300	31 March	Journal	80
		300			300
			31 March	Balance b/d	300

Closing inventory

Inventory – statement of financial position

	£		£
31 March Journal	5,200		

Inventory – income statement

	£			£
		31 March	Journal	5,200

Once all of the ledger accounts have been updated for the journal adjustments then a new final trial balance is drawn up which reflects all of the error corrections and adjustments. This is the one that will be used to prepare the financial statements so take great care to ensure to include:

- All the updated balances and
- All the new balances that have come from the adjustments.

You will find that you have three inventory account balances but do not worry about this at the moment as it will be explained when we prepare the financial statements.

Final trial balance as at 31 March 20X9

	Debit £	Credit £
Buildings at cost	100,000	
Furniture and fittings at cost	4,800	
Motor vehicles at cost	32,700	
Computer at cost	2,850	
Accumulated depreciation – buildings		6,000
Accumulated depreciation – furniture and fittings		2,880
Accumulated depreciation – motor vehicles		15,305
Accumulated depreciation – computer		1,900
Inventory	4,400	
Bank	3,960	
Petty cash	100	
Sales ledger control	15,000	
Purchases ledger control		5,010
Capital		130,000
Sales		155,020
Sales returns	2,100	
Purchases	80,200	
Purchases returns		1,300
Bank charges	200	
Discounts allowed	1,060	
Discounts received		1,260
Wages	32,780	
Rates	6,000	
Telephone	1,140	
Electricity	1,480	
Insurance	1,200	
Motor expenses	1,380	
Office expenses	1,160	
Allowance for doubtful debts		300
VAT		820
Drawings	15,800	
Suspense	–	
Depreciation expense – building	2,000	
Depreciation expense – furniture and fittings	960	
Depreciation expense – motor vehicles	7,455	
Depreciation expense – computer	950	
Accruals		500
Prepayments	300	
Irrecoverable debts expense	240	
Allowance for doubtful debts adjustment	80	
Inventory – statement of financial position	5,200	
Inventory – income statement		5,200
	325,495	325,495

Preparing the financial statements

Step 5   The next stage is to determine which of the balances in the final trial balance are income statement (IS) balances and which are statement of financial position (SFP) balances.

This was covered in Chapter 1 and we will just list each balance as either IS or SFP in this exercise.

Final trial balance as at 31 March 20X9

	Debit £	Credit £	IS or SFP
Buildings at cost	100,000		SFP
Furniture and fittings at cost	4,800		SFP
Motor vehicles at cost	32,700		SFP
Computer at cost	2,850		SFP
Accumulated depreciation – buildings		6,000	SFP
Accumulated depreciation – furniture and fittings		2,880	SFP
Accumulated depreciation – motor vehicles		15,305	SFP
Accumulated depreciation – computer		1,900	SFP
Inventory	4,400		IS
Bank	3,960		SFP
Petty cash	100		SFP
Sales ledger control	15,000		SFP
Purchases ledger control		5,010	SFP
Capital		130,000	SFP
Sales		155,020	IS
Sales returns	2,100		IS
Purchases	80,200		IS
Purchases returns		1,300	IS
Bank charges	200		IS
Discounts allowed	1,060		IS
Discounts received		1,260	IS
Wages	32,780		IS
Rates	6,000		IS
Telephone	1,140		IS
Electricity	1,480		IS
Insurance	1,200		IS
Motor expenses	1,380		IS
Office expenses	1,160		IS
Allowance for doubtful debts		300	SFP
VAT		820	SFP
Drawings	15,800		SFP
Suspense	–	–	–
Dep'n expense – building	2,000		IS
Dep'n expense – furniture & fittings	960		IS
Dep'n expense – motor vehicles	7,455		IS
Dep'n expense – computer	950		IS

	Debit £	Credit £	IS or SFP
Accruals		500	SFP
Prepayments	300		SFP
Irrecoverable debts expense	240		IS
Allowance for doubtful debts adjustment	80		IS
Inventory – SFP	5,200		SFP
Inventory – IS		5,200	IS
	325,495	325,495	

Financial statements

Step 6   The final stage is now to take each of the ledger balances and present them in the correct place in the financial statements.

John Thompson

Income statement for the year ending 31 March 20X9

	Notes	£	£
Sales revenue			155,020
Less: sales returns			(2,100)
	1		152,920
Cost of sales			
Opening inventory		4,400	
Purchases		80,200	
Less: purchases returns		(1,300)	
	1	83,300	
Less: closing inventory		(5,200)	
			(78,100)
Gross profit			74,820
Discounts received	2		1,260
			76,080
Less: expenses			
Bank charges		200	
Discounts allowed		1,060	
Wages		32,780	
Rates		6,000	
Telephone		1,140	
Electricity		1,480	
Insurance		1,200	
Motor expenses		1,380	
Office expenses		1,160	
Depreciation – building		2,000	
furniture and fittings		960	
motor vehicles		7,455	
computer		950	
Allowance for doubtful debts adjustments		80	

	Notes	£	£
Irrecoverable debts expense		240	
			(58,085)
Profit for the year			17,995

Notes

1 Sales returns and purchases returns have been netted off from sales and purchases respectively

2 Discounts received have been shown as miscellaneous income under gross profit.

Statement of financial position as at 31 March 20X9

	Cost £	Accumulated depreciation £	Carrying amount £
Non-current assets			
Building	100,000	6,000	94,000
Furniture and fittings	4,800	2,880	1,920
Motor vehicles	32,700	15,305	17,395
Computer	2,850	1,900	950
	140,350	26,085	114,265
Current assets			
Inventory		5,200	
Receivables	15,000		
Less: allowance	(300)		
		14,700	
Prepayments		300	
Bank		3,960	
Cash		100	
		24,260	
Current liabilities			
Payables	5,010		
VAT	820		
Accruals	500		
		(6,330)	
Net current assets			17,930
			132,195
Financed by:			
Capital at 1 April 20X8			130,000
Profit for the year			17,995
			147,995
Less: drawings			(15,800)
Capital at 31 March 20X9			132,195

Closing off and clearing the final ledger accounts

Once the balances on the trial balance have been taken to the income statement and statement of financial position there is one final set of adjustments that must be done to some of the ledger accounts.

Step 7 **The income and expense ledger accounts must be closed off or cleared as the balances are no longer required in the general ledger.**

This is done by taking the balances on each individual income and expense ledger account to a new ledger account known as the INCOME STATEMENT LEDGER ACCOUNT.

HOW IT WORKS

The final balances on the sales account, purchases account and wages account are shown below.

Sales

	£		£
		Balance b/d	155,020

Purchases

	£		£
Balance b/d	80,200		

Wages

	£		£
Balance b/d	32,780		

These accounts must now be closed off ready to start with a clean sheet at the start of the next accounting period. This is done by transferring the balances remaining to an income statement ledger account.

Sales

	£		£
Income statement	155,020	Balance b/d	155,020

Purchases

	£		£
Balance b/d	80,200	Income statement	80,200

Wages

	£		£
Balance b/d	32,780	Income statement	32,780

Income statement

	£		£
Purchases	80,200	Sales	155,020
Wages	32,780		

This will be done for all income statement balances and there will need to be journal entries for each of these final adjustments. Therefore, the final set of journal entries in full will be as follows:

Journal entries

	Debit £	Credit £
Opening inventory		
Income statement	4,400	
Inventory		4,400
Sales		
Sales	155,020	
Income statement		155,020
Sales returns		
Income statement	2,100	
Sales returns		2,100
Purchases		
Income statement	80,200	
Purchases		80,200
Purchases returns		
Purchases returns	1,300	
Income statement		1,300
Bank charges		
Income statement	200	
Bank charges		200
Discounts allowed		
Income statement	1,060	
Discounts allowed		1,060
Discounts received		
Discounts received	1,260	
Income statement		1,260
Wages		
Income statement	32,780	
Wages		32,780

	Debit £	Credit £
Rates		
Income statement	6,000	
Rates		6,000
Telephone		
Income statement	1,140	
Telephone		1,140
Electricity		
Income statement	1,480	
Electricity		1,480
Insurance		
Income statement	1,200	
Insurance		1,200
Motor expenses		
Income statement	1,380	
Motor expenses		1,380
Office expenses		
Income statement	1,160	
Office expenses		1,160
Depreciation expense – buildings		
Income statement	2,000	
Dep'n expense – buildings		2,000
Depreciation expense – furniture and fittings		
Income statement	960	
Dep'n expense – furniture and fittings		960
Depreciation expense – motor vehicles		
Income statement	7,455	
Dep'n expense – motor vehicles		7,455
Depreciation expense – computer		
Income statement	950	
Dep'n expense – computer		950
Irrecoverable debt expense		
Income statement	240	
Irrecoverable debt expense		240
Allowance for doubtful debts adjustment		
Income statement	80	
Allowance for doubtful debts adjustment		80
Inventory – income statement		
Inventory – income statement	5,200	
Income statement		5,200

The income statement ledger account will look like this when all these journals are processed:

Income statement

	£		£
Opening inventory	4,400	Sales	155,020
Sales returns	2,100	Purchases returns	1,300
Purchases	80,200	Discounts received	1,260
Bank charges	200	Closing inventory	5,200
Discounts allowed	1,060		
Wages	32,780		
Rates	6,000		
Telephone	1,140		
Electricity	1,480		
Insurance	1,200		
Motor expenses	1,380		
Office expenses	1,160		
Dep'n – buildings	2,000		
Dep'n – F&F	960		
Dep'n – motor vehicles	7,455		
Dep'n – computer	950		
Irrecoverable debts	240		
Allowance for doubtful debts adjustment	80		

There is no need to do any similar adjustments to statement of financial position assets and liabilities ledger accounts. They remain as opening balances for the following accounting period in the ledger account. For example the closing balance on the Buildings at cost account is £100,000 and this remains as the opening balance for the buildings at the start of the next accounting period.

However, as the very last stage of the process the drawings account and the income statement ledger account need to be cleared to the capital account. The figure carried down in this is the opening balance of capital for the new period, while there are no figures carried down on either the income statement ledger account or the drawings account.

The closing journal would be as follows:

	Debit £	Credit £
Income statement		
Income statement	17,995	
Capital		17,995
Drawings		
Capital	15,800	
Drawings		15,800

The three ledger accounts would be as follows:

Income statement

	£		£
Opening inventory	4,400	Sales	155,020
Sales returns	2,100	Purchases returns	1,300
Purchases	80,200	Discounts received	1,260
Bank charges	200	Closing inventory	5,200
Discounts allowed	1,060		
Wages	32,780		
Rates	6,000		
Telephone	1,140		
Electricity	1,480		
Insurance	1,200		
Motor expenses	1,380		
Office expenses	1,160		
Dep'n – buildings	2,000		
Dep'n – F&F	960		
Dep'n – motor vehicles	7,455		
Dep'n – computer	950		
Irrecoverable debts	240		
Allowance for doubtful debts adjustment	80		
Capital	17,995		
	162,780		162,780

Capital

		£			£
31 Mar	Drawings	15,800	31 Mar	Balance b/d	130,000
31 Mar	Balance c/d	132,195	31 Mar	Income statement	17,995
		147,995			147,995
			1 Apr	Balance b/d	132,195

Drawings

		£			£
31 Mar	Balance b/d	15,800	31 Mar	Capital	15,800

Note that the balance brought down on the capital account at the beginning of the new period is the statement of financial position total that we saw on the statement of financial position. It is the amount of the investment that the owner retains in the business, represented by the business's assets less its liabilities.

Task 3

What are the year end journal entries required to clear the following accounts?

(a)   Purchases returns account

DEBIT

CREDIT

(b)   Insurance account

DEBIT

CREDIT

(c)   Sales ledger control account

DEBIT

CREDIT

THE COST OF GOODS SOLD ACCOUNT

An alternative method of ledger accounting for the figures that comprise cost of sales in the income statement is to maintain one ledger account for COST OF GOODS SOLD which contains:

- The brought down figure for opening inventory, plus
- Purchases for the period, less
- Purchases returns in the period, less
- Closing inventory at the end of the period.

This method means that the closing inventory adjustment is a debit to the statement of financial position and a credit to the cost of goods sold account.

HOW IT WORKS

If John Thompson maintained a cost of goods sold account, the process would have worked as follows:

Step 1   **Bring down the opening balance on the cost of goods sold account, being the opening inventory balance.**

Step 2   **Post purchases and purchases returns amounts to the cost of goods sold account.**

Cost of goods sold

		£			£
31 Mar	Balance b/d	4,400	31 Mar	Purchases returns	1,300
31 Mar	Purchases	80,200			

The balance on this account – £83,300 – will appear on the initial trial balance in place of the three accounts for opening inventory, purchases and purchases returns.

Step 3   **Prepare the year end inventory adjustment journal and post it:**

	Debit £	Credit £
Inventory – statement of financial position	5,200	
Cost of goods sold		5,200

Cost of goods sold

		£			£
31 Mar	Balance b/d	4,400	31 Mar	Purchases returns	1,300
31 Mar	Purchases	80,200	31 Mar	Journal	5,200

Step 4   **Clear balance to income statement ledger account:**

Cost of goods sold

		£			£
31 Mar	Balance b/d	4,400	31 Mar	Purchases returns	1,300
31 Mar	Purchases	80,200	31 Mar	Journal	5,200
			31 Mar	Income statement	78,100
		84,600			84,600

Note that the balance on the account which is cleared to the income statement ledger – £78,100 – is the same figure that was shown in the income statement for cost of sales.

Task 4

In a trading period a business makes sales of £45,200. Opening inventory was £2,500 and closing inventory was £1,400. Purchases amounted to £22,360, sales returns £850 and purchase returns £430.

What was the gross profit for the period?

£ [ ]

CHAPTER OVERVIEW

- An individual who is the only owner of a business which is not a company is a sole trader. For accounting purposes the individual and the business are treated as separate entities

- The income statement shows the income and expenses of the business for an accounting period. The statement of financial position shows the assets and liabilities of the business at the end of the accounting period

- The amount owed back to the sole trader by the business is shown in the capital section of the statement of financial position. The total capital owed to the owner is the amount they have paid into the business plus the profit earned less drawings taken out of the business. This is also the same figure as the net assets of the business, shown in the top section of the statement of financial position.

- The financial statements for a sole trader are prepared as follows:

  - Step 1: Transfer all of the closing balances on the ledger accounts to the trial balance. If it does not balance, create a suspense account and investigate the reason for the errors

  - Step 2: Prepare journal entries to correct any errors identified and to clear the suspense account

  - Step 3: Prepare journal entries for the period end adjustments for depreciation, accruals, prepayments, irrecoverable and doubtful debts and closing inventory

  - Step 4: Update the ledger account balances for the adjustments and corrections and prepare a final trial balance

  - Step 5: Determine which of the balances in the trial balance are income statement balances and which are statement of financial position balances

  - Step 6: Transfer the balances from the trial balance to the financial statements

  - Step 7: As a final year end adjustment, clear out all income and expense balances to the income statement ledger account, and then clear out the income statement ledger account and drawings balances to the capital account

Keywords

Sole trader – A business which is not a company that is owned by one individual

Drawings – cash and goods that the owner of a business takes out of the business for his/her own use

Income statement ledger account – the ledger account to which all income and expense ledger accounts are cleared at the end of the accounting period

TEST YOUR LEARNING

Test 1

A sole trader had a balance on her capital account of £34,560 on 1 July 20X7. During the year ending 30 June 20X8 she made a net profit of £48,752 but withdrew £49,860 from the business. What is the capital balance at 30 June 20X8?

£ [   ]

Test 2

The owner of a business took goods from inventory for his own use which had originally cost £1,500 and which had a selling price of £2,100. What are the two alternative double entry accounting treatments for this transaction?

(a)

DEBIT [   ]

CREDIT [   ]

(b)

DEBIT [   ]

CREDIT [   ]

Test 3

The telephone expense and insurance expense accounts of a sole trader have balances of £3,400 and £1,600 respectively at 30 September 20X8. However £300 of telephone expense is to be accrued and £200 of insurance has been prepaid. What are the final expense figures that will appear in the income statement for the year?

Telephone expense	£	
Insurance expense	£	

Test 4

A sole trader has the following balances in her initial trial balance at 31 May 20X8:

	£
Furniture and fittings at cost	12,600
Motor vehicles at cost	38,500
Accumulated depreciation at 1 June 20X7:	
– Furniture and fittings	3,400
– Motor vehicles	15,500

Furniture and fittings are depreciated at the rate of 20% per annum on cost and motor vehicles are depreciated on the reducing balance basis at a rate of 30%.

Complete the table below to show the total carrying amount of the non-current assets that will appear in the statement of financial position at 31 May 20X8.

Non-current assets			
	Cost	Accumulated depreciation	Carrying amount
	£	£	£
Furniture and fittings			
Motor vehicles			

Test 5

Given below is the list of balances taken from a sole trader's ledger accounts at 30 June 20X8.

	£
Sales	308,000
Machinery at cost	67,400
Office equipment at cost	5,600
Office costs	2,300
Distribution costs	4,100
Sales ledger control	38,400
Telephone expenses	1,800
Purchases ledger control	32,100
Heat and light	3,100
Bank overdraft	3,600
Purchases	196,000
Petty cash	100
Insurance	4,200
Accumulated depreciation – machinery	31,200
Accumulated depreciation – office equipment	3,300
Inventory at 1 July 20X7	16,500
Loan from bank	10,000
Miscellaneous expenses	2,200
Wages	86,700
Loan interest	600
Capital	60,000
Drawings	20,000
Allowance for doubtful debts	1,000

The following information is also available:

(i)   After drawing up the initial trial balance the bookkeeper spotted that the heat and light account had been undercast by £200

(ii)   The value of inventory at 30 June 20X8 was £18,000

(iii) The machinery and office equipment have yet to be depreciated for the year. Machinery is depreciated at 30% on the reducing balance basis and office equipment at 20% of cost

(iv)   £200 of loan interest has yet to be paid for the year and a telephone bill for £400 for the three months to 30 June 20X8 did not arrive until after the trial balance had been drawn up

(v)   Of the insurance payments £800 is for the year ending 30 September 20X8

(vi)   An irrecoverable debt of £1,200 is to be written off and an allowance of £1,116 is required against the remaining receivables

You are required to:

(a)   Draw up an initial trial balance and set up any suspense account required

(b)   Prepare journal entries to clear the suspense account and make all of the year end adjustments required from the information in the question

(c)   Update the ledger accounts for the journal entries

(d)   Prepare an income statement for the year ending 30 June 20X8 and statement of financial position at that date

chapter 3:
INCOMPLETE RECORDS

chapter coverage 📖

Many small businesses do not keep the types of accounting record that we saw in Accounts Preparation I, such as books of prime entry, ledger accounts in general and memorandum ledgers, and asset registers. They do however keep some of the primary records for the business, such as invoices, credit notes, remittance advices, cheque book and paying in book stubs and petty cash receipts. If a business only keeps some of these primary records then it is said to have INCOMPLETE RECORDS. From these it is possible to find missing information and then to reconstruct the figures needed for the business's financial statements.

The topics we cover in this chapter are:

✍ What is meant by incomplete records

✍ Using the accounting equation

✍ Reconstructing the cash and bank accounts

✍ Reconstructing the receivables and payables accounts

✍ Using mark ups and profit margins

✍ The approach to follow for incomplete records tasks

✍ Finding a missing inventory value

WHAT ARE INCOMPLETE RECORDS?

Many small businesses do not keep full accounting records made up of books of prime entry, ledger accounts in general and memorandum ledgers, asset registers, monthly reconciliations and trial balances. They may not have the time or resources, so instead they just keep the basic primary records necessary to keep track of the transactions of the business. A typical small business may have the following information from which details of the transactions can be determined:

- Bank statements, paying in book stubs, cheque book stubs
- Copies of sales invoices and maybe credit notes sent out to customers
- Purchase invoices and credit notes received from suppliers
- Receipts for purchases made in cash
- Lists of customers who have not yet paid – receivables
- Lists of suppliers who have not yet been paid – payables

A business may have only limited amounts of information because it has suffered some sort of disaster, for example:

- Theft or loss of records or loss of assets such as cash or inventory

- Fire or flood leading to damage to records or assets

Finally a business may find that there are inconsistencies between the records that it does have, for example:

- Physical non-current assets not agreeing with general ledger balances and/or the asset register

- A physical inventory count failing to agree with the records of receipts into and out of inventory

- The bank statement not reconciling with the cash book, even after all authentic transactions and timing differences have been taken into account

- The balances on purchases ledger accounts not reconciling with supplier statements

In all these scenarios the information available to the business is either inadequate or missing, that is there are INCOMPLETE RECORDS.

However limited the primary records are, or the other available information is, the owner of the business will still want to know how much profit or loss has been made in the year and what assets and liabilities they have at the end of the year.

This is where an accountant is required, to piece together the information so they can prepare:

- An income statement to show how much profit or loss was made in the accounting period and

- A statement of financial position listing the business's assets and liabilities at the end of the period.

Several techniques are available to the accountant to reconstruct the figures that are needed. Each of these will be considered in turn:

- The accounting equation – assets minus liabilities (net assets) equals capital
- Reconstruction of the cash/bank account
- Use of receivables and payables accounts
- Use of mark-ups and margins

THE ACCOUNTING EQUATION

Manipulating the components of the accounting equation can be very useful when preparing some figures in the financial statements when records are incomplete. Remember:

| ASSETS | – | LIABILITIES | = | CAPITAL |

Assets minus liabilities (ie capital) at any point in time are known as the NET ASSETS of the business.

Calculating opening (and closing) capital

To prepare the financial statements of a business with incomplete records we may need to determine the opening capital balance, that is the balance brought down at the beginning of the accounting period. This can be done by calculating net assets at the start of the period.

HOW IT WORKS

Stan Kelly runs a small business. He does not keep any books of prime entry or ledger accounts but he can provide you with information about the assets and liabilities of his business:

He has only two non-current assets – a car and a computer

He can easily determine the value of his inventory at any time.

He keeps copies of all of his sales invoices and marks each one as paid when the customer sends a cheque, so he knows exactly what the receivables position is – the unmarked invoices.

He keeps all of his suppliers' invoices and marks them as paid when he sends out a cheque to the supplier so his payables are any unmarked invoices.

BPP
LEARNING MEDIA

Stan has an accounting year that runs to 31 March each year and he has provided you with the following information on his assets and liabilities:

	31 March 20X8 £	31 March 20X9 £
Car – valuation (see note below)	7,000	6,000
Computer – valuation (see note below)	3,000	2,500
Inventory	7,300	8,900
Receivables	10,500	11,200
Payables for purchases	6,400	5,200
Payables for expenses	400	200
Bank	1,200	1,800
Cash in till	100	100

As these are all the assets and liabilities that Stan has, we can easily determine his opening capital balance by finding the total of assets minus liabilities (his net assets) at 31 March 20X8.

Note: Business accounts should normally include non-current assets, such as the car and computer, at their cost less an amount for accumulated depreciation ie carrying amount. However as this information may not be available in an incomplete records situation it is reasonable to include the assets at their current valuation, being the best estimate of their carrying amount.

Statement of assets and liabilities at 1 April 20X8

	£
Car	7,000
Computer	3,000
Inventory	7,300
Receivables	10,500
Payables for purchases	(6,400)
Payables for expenses	(400)
Bank	1,200
Cash in till	100
Opening capital as at 1 April 20X8 = net assets	22,300

The same technique can be used to calculate closing capital at the end of the accounting period.

Task 1

What is Stan's closing capital balance at 31 March 20X9?

£ [   ]

Calculating profit, drawings or capital introduced

The closing capital balance can be analysed in another way however, not as net assets but as:

> **CLOSING CAPITAL =**
>
> **OPENING CAPITAL + CAPITAL INTRODUCED + PROFIT – DRAWINGS**

If net assets of the business have increased then the closing capital balance must be larger than the opening capital balance. This must have been caused either:

- By capital being introduced and/or
- By more profit being made than drawings being taken.

This presentation of the accounting equation can also be written as:

> **INCREASE IN NET ASSETS =**
>
> CAPITAL INTRODUCED + PROFIT – DRAWINGS

HOW IT WORKS

We know Stan Kelly's opening capital balance is £22,300 and (from Task 1) that his closing capital balance is £25,100. There has therefore been an increase in capital of £2,800 in the period:

	£
Net assets at 1 April 20X8	22,300
Net assets at 31 March 20X9	25,100
Increase in net assets	2,800

Stan has told you that he has not paid in any additional capital to the business during the year. From his bank statements and cheque book stubs you know that his drawings were £15,700 during the year. We can now use the accounting equation.

> **CAPITAL INTRODUCED + PROFIT – DRAWINGS =**
>
> INCREASE IN NET ASSETS

in order to find the missing figure – ie the profit for the year.

	£
Capital introduced	0
Profit	?
Drawings	(15,700)
Increase in net assets	2,800

To calculate the missing profit figure, we add the figure for drawings to the figure for the increase in net assets: £2,800 + £15,700 = £18,500. Check that it works:

	£
Capital introduced	0
Profit	18,500
Drawings	(15,700)
Increase in net assets	2,800

The calculation can also be made using the capital ledger account:

Capital

	£		£
Drawings	15,700	Balance b/d (opening net assets)	22,300
Balance c/d (closing net assets)	25,100		?

You can see immediately that the account does not add up – there is a missing figure on the credit side. This will be the amount of profit made in the period. If we balance the account then we can find this missing figure.

Capital

	£		£
Drawings	15,700	Balance b/d (opening net assets)	22,300
Balance c/d (closing net assets)	25,100	Profit for the year	18,500
	40,800		40,800

Task 2

A small business has opening net assets of £31,400 and closing net assets of £40,600. The owner tells you that he has paid an additional £5,000 of capital into the business during the year and his income has exceeded his expenses by £14,400, but he failed to keep a record of the drawings he made from the business for his living expenses.

What drawings did the owner make during the year?

£ [   ]

CASH AND BANK ACCOUNT

While using the accounting equation allows us to calculate the total profit made in a year by a business, it gives no details of how this profit is made up. We can only find this by looking at the actual transactions of the business in more detail. The place to start when trying to reconstruct transactions is the cash and bank account movements.

HOW IT WORKS

Maria Donald runs a small business selling computer accessories, largely on credit but with some cash sales. You have access to her bank statements, paying-in slip stubs, cheque stubs and till rolls for the year to 31 December 20X8 and have summarised the transactions that have taken place as follows:

Till summary

Money paid into the till – per till rolls	£4,200

Bank account summary

Receipts

Cash paid into the bank account from the till	£3,600
Cheques paid into the bank from credit customers	£48,700

Payments

Cheques written to pay credit suppliers	£37,600
Cheques written to pay other expenses	£4,100

Maria tells you that she always keeps a float of £100 in the till. You discover from the bank statements that the bank balance on 1 January 20X8 was £650 in credit and that on 31 December 20X8 it was £720 in credit. The figures that Maria cannot however tell you are her drawings:

- How much cash she took out of the till and

- How much she withdrew from the bank account via automated teller machines (ATMs).

First we need to reconstruct the cash account (effectively the till account) to determine her cash drawings.

Cash account

	£		£
Balance b/d	100	Cash paid into the bank	3,600
Money paid into the till	4,200		?
		Balance c/d	100

You can see immediately that the account does not add up – there is a missing figure on the credit side. This will be the amount of cash Maria took out of the till as drawings. If we balance the account then we can find this missing figure.

Cash account

	£		£
Balance b/d	100	Cash paid into the bank	3,600
Money paid into the till	4,200	Drawings	600
		Balance c/d	100
	4,300		4,300

We will do the same reconstruction with the bank account:

Bank account

	£		£
Balance b/d	650	Cheques to credit suppliers	37,600
Cash paid into bank	3,600	Cheques for expenses	4,100
Cheques paid into bank	48,700		?
		Balance c/d	720

Again the account does not add up as there is a missing credit entry – drawings from the bank account via ATMs. Balance the account to find this missing figure:

Bank account

	£		£
Balance b/d	650	Cheques to credit suppliers	37,600
Cash paid into bank	3,600	Cheques for expenses	4,100
Cheques paid into bank	48,700	Drawings	10,530
		Balance c/d	720
	52,950		52,950

Therefore Maria's total drawings for the year are:

	£
Cash drawings	600
Bank drawings	10,530
	11,130

As we saw in API, the cash and bank accounts are often drawn up together in a single three-column cash ledger account. Here is how a three column cash book would look for Maria:

Cash and bank account							
	Disc	Cash	Bank		Disc	Cash	Bank
	all'd £	£	£		rec'd £	£	£
	£				£		
Balance b/d		100	650	Cash paid in		3,600	
Money paid in		4,200		Payables			37,600
Cash paid in			3,600	Expenses			4,100
Cheques paid in			48,700	Drawings		600	10,530
				Balance c/d		100	720
		4,300	52,950			4,300	52,950

The important point to note here is the double entry between the cash and the bank columns. The cash paid into the bank must have come out of the till so the bank account is debited and the cash account is credited with the £3,600 of bankings.

RECONSTRUCTING RECEIVABLES ACCOUNT AND PAYABLES ACCOUNT

We have seen how to reconstruct the cash and bank accounts from information that we can find in the business and how to use these accounts to find a missing figure, such as drawings. Now we will reconstruct the receivables account and payables account in order to find missing figures for sales and purchases respectively.

HOW IT WORKS

Maria Donald has now provided you with information about her receivables and payables at 31 December 20X7 and 31 December 20X8.

	31 Dec 20X7 £	31 Dec 20X8 £
Receivables	4,500	4,800
Payables for purchases	3,900	3,100
Payables for expenses	400	700

From the bank account we know that £48,700 was received from receivables during the year and £37,600 was paid to payables for purchases. Take care that you do not confuse these receipts and payments with the sales and purchases for the year. As there are opening and closing receivables and payables these cash movements are not the sales and purchases – the cash figures must be adjusted for the opening and closing balances. This is done most easily by reconstructing a receivables and payables account.

Receivables account

	£		£
Balance b/d	4,500	Receipts from receivables	48,700
	?	Balance c/d	4,800

Clearly the account has a large missing figure – this will be the sales made on credit – the double entry being a debit in the receivables account and a credit to the sales account. If we balance the account we can find the missing figure for sales on credit.

Receivables account

	£		£
Balance b/d	4,500	Receipts from receivables	48,700
Sales on credit	49,000	Balance c/d	4,800
	53,500		53,500

We now know that sales on credit totalled £49,000. Remember however that Maria also has a till and the cash account shows that the receipts into the till were £4,200. These must be sales for cash – therefore the total sales for the year are:

	£
Credit sales	49,000
Cash sales	4,200
	53,200

In this example the only entries in the receivables account were the opening and closing balances and the cash receipts from receivables – if there were discounts allowed to customers and/or irrecoverable debts written off and/or contra entries they must also be entered onto the credit side of the account before finding the balance.

Now we will do the same for credit purchases using the payables account:

Payables account

	£		£
Payments to payables	37,600	Balance b/d	3,900
Balance c/d	3,100		?

Again there is a large missing figure – the credit purchases – which can be found by balancing the account and finding the purchases as the balancing figure.

Payables account

	£		£
Payments to payables	37,600	Opening balance	3,900
Closing balance	3,100	Purchases on credit	36,800
	40,700		40,700

The credit purchases are £36,800 – the full double entry would be a debit in the purchases account and this credit in the payables account.

Finally we can do the same for the expenses – the payment out of the bank account was £4,100 but as there are opening and closing payables for expenses this is not the expenses total – we need to set up an expenses account to adjust the cash payment.

Expenses account

	£		£
Payment from bank	4,100	Balance b/d	400
Balance c/d	700		?

The missing figure will be the expenses incurred for the period.

Expenses account

	£		£
Payment from bank	4,100	Balance b/d	400
Balance c/d	700	Expenses	4,400
	4,800		4,800

Task 3

A business has opening receivables of £3,300 and had receipts from receivables of £38,700 during the year. At the end of the year it was decided that one debt of £300 was to be written off and closing receivables after the write off were £2,800.

What are the credit sales for the year?

£ [   ]

Using these ledger accounts

As you can see, each of these ledger accounts has four main entries. (There may be others such as discounts but these are the main ones):

- Opening balance (balance b/d)
- Closing balance (balance c/d)
- Cash paid/received
- Sales/purchases/expenses

Provided that you know three of these four figures you can always determine the final one by finding the balance on the account. In these examples we had to find sales, purchases and expenses. However the missing figure could also be the closing balance on the account or the cash paid/received. As long as you know the other three figures then this is possible.

Task 4

A business has opening payables of £4,100 and closing payables of £3,600. The owner of the business knows that the credit purchases for the year totalled £40,000.

How much was paid to payables during the year?

£ [   ]

Preparing the income statement

Having reconstructed the receivables and payables accounts we now have the key income statement figures – sales and purchases as well as expenses. The only figures now required are the opening and closing inventory and then the income statement can be completed.

HOW IT WORKS

Maria now informs you that her opening and closing inventories were as follows:

	31 Dec 20X7 £	31 Dec 20X8 £
Inventory	3,000	4,000

We will now prepare Maria's income statement for the year to 31 December 20X8:

	£	£
Sales revenue		53,200
Less: cost of sales		
opening inventory	3,000	
Purchases	36,800	
	39,800	
Less: closing inventory	(4,000)	
		(35,800)
Gross profit		17,400
Less: expenses		(4,400)
Profit for the year		13,000

Preparing the statement of financial position

The top part of the statement of financial position is simply a list of the assets and liabilities of the business at the end of the year. These can be found by searching through the information and listing each of the assets and liabilities.

The bottom part of the statement of financial position is made up of:

	£
Opening capital	X
Add: profit	X
	X
Less: drawings	(X)
	X

- The opening capital can be found using the accounting equation (assets less liabilities = capital); if the assets and liabilities at the start of the year are totalled then this is the opening capital.

- The profit figure is the profit for the year from the income statement.

- The drawings may be given in the information or you may have to determine them by reconstructing the cash/bank account.

HOW IT WORKS

If we look back at the information that Maria has given us we can first list the assets and liabilities at the start of the year to give the opening capital balance.

	31 Dec 20X7 £
Cash	100
Bank	650
Receivables	4,500
Payables for purchases	(3,900)
Payables for expenses	(400)
Inventory	3,000
Opening capital	3,950

We have the profit figure from the income statement and the drawings were calculated from the cash and bank accounts. Now we can list the assets and liabilities at the end of the year and prepare Maria's statement of financial position.

Statement of financial position at 31 December 20X8

	£	£
Current assets:		
Inventory		4,000
Receivables		4,800
Bank		720
Cash		100
		9,620
Current liabilities:		
Payables for purchases	3,100	
Payables for expenses	700	
		(3,800)
		5,820
Opening capital		3,950
Add: profit (from the income statement)		13,000
		16,950
Less: drawings (from the cash and bank accounts)		(11,130)
		5,820

The accounts for Maria have now been completed by piecing together the information that we do have and using the three techniques learned so far:

- Using the accounting equation
- Reconstructing the bank and cash accounts
- Reconstructing receivables and payables accounts

USE OF MARK-UPS AND MARGINS

In a shop the owner is likely to know how he/she prices the goods for sale. They will normally take the cost of the goods and add a percentage to reach the selling price of the goods. This difference between the cost and the selling price is the GROSS PROFIT or MARGIN, and it can be used in an incomplete records situation to find either the sales figure or the cost of sales figure.

Profit mark-up

A PROFIT MARK-UP is a percentage of the cost of the goods that is added to the cost in order to reach the sales price.

HOW IT WORKS

A retailer uses a 20% mark-up on cost to fix the selling price. The cost of the goods being sold is £150. What is the selling price?

This can first be determined using percentages, known as the COST STRUCTURE:

	%
Sales	
Cost	
Gross profit	

As this is a mark-up on cost the cost figure is put in as 100% – the mark-up is 20% so the sales percentage is 120%.

	%
Sales	120
Cost	100
Gross profit	20

Now we add in the figure that we know for cost:

	%	£
Sales	120	
Cost	100	150
Gross profit	20	

If this £150 is equivalent to 100% then the sales of 120% must be:

$$£150 \times \frac{120}{100} = £180$$

We can now complete the figures for sales and gross profit:

	%	£
Sales	120	180
Cost	100	150
Gross profit	20	30

Alternatively you could have been told that the sales were £180 and required to find the cost of these sales.

	%	£
Sales	120	180
Cost	100	
Gross profit	20	

Using the cost structure the sales figure of £180 is equivalent to 120% so the cost can be calculated as:

$$£180 \times \frac{100}{120} = £150$$

Task 5

A business operates with a mark-up on cost of 30%. The sales for a period were £1,950.

What is the cost of the goods sold? $\frac{30}{100} \times 1950$

£ [   ]

Profit margin

A PROFIT MARGIN is gross profit expressed as a percentage of the sales figure.

HOW IT WORKS

A retailer operates with a profit margin of 30%. His sales for the period are £1,200. What is the cost of those sales?

Set up the cost structure – as profit margin is a percentage of sales value, this time it is the sales figure that is 100%:

	%
Sales	100
Cost	70
Gross profit	30

If the gross profit is to be 30% of sales then the cost of the sales must be 70%.

Now put in the figure that you know:

	%	£
Sales	100	1,200
Cost	70	
Gross profit	30	

Use the cost structure to determine the missing figures. If sales are £1,200 then cost must be:

$$£1,200 \times \frac{70}{100} = £840$$

	%	£
Sales	100	1,200
Cost	70	840
Gross profit	30	360

Alternatively you might have been told that the cost of sales was £840 and asked to find the sales figure:

$$£840 \times \frac{100}{70} = £1,200$$

Task 6

A business operates with a profit margin of 40%. The cost of the goods sold in a period was £2,000.

What were the sales for the period?

Sales 100
Profit 40
Cost 60
$\frac{100}{60} \times 2000$

£ [   ]

APPROACH TO INCOMPLETE RECORD TASKS

Incomplete records tasks can at first appear to be very daunting, however with practice you will become familiar with the approach to follow and the techniques to use.

Remember that you have a variety of techniques to choose from:

- Accounting equation
- Cash/bank account reconstruction
- Receivables/payables accounts reconstruction
- Mark-up/margin

If you are given information about the mark-up or profit margin in an assessment then you will need to use it – so if you think you can find the sales or cost of sales figures without the cost structure you have gone wrong somewhere!

You need a clear and logical approach to these tasks and the following steps may be useful:

Step 1	Read through the information to get a feel for what you have been given.
Step 2	Decide whether or not you need to reconstruct the three column cash book, or just the cash account or the bank account – in many tasks you are given a neat summary of the bank transactions and therefore there is no need to include this in your answer. However you may not get the same detail for cash transactions.
Step 3	Set up the receivables and payables accounts and put in the opening and closing balances.
Step 4	Set up the cost structure in percentages if you are given a mark-up or a margin. You should also set up a working for the trading account, showing sales, cost of sales (broken down into opening and closing inventory and purchases) and gross profit.
Step 5	Work carefully through the task entering each figure in the working ledger accounts, the cost structure and the trading account. Take special care with the cash and bank transactions – this is only one side of the double entry and the other side of the transaction must also be entered. For example payment of a credit supplier from the bank account must be debited to the payables account, and the receipt of money from receivables must be entered as a credit in the receivables account.
Step 6	When you have entered as many figures as you can, take a look at what you have in the working ledger accounts and cost structure to determine how you can find the figures that are missing.

HOW IT WORKS

Jack Eagle runs a small business selling his goods on credit at a profit margin of 25%. He does not keep proper accounting records but has produced a summary of his bank statements for the year to 31 March 20X9.

Bank statement summary

	£
Opening balance – 1 April 20X8	380
Receipt from bank as loan	5,000
Receipts from receivables	61,200
	66,580
Payments for expenses	(2,100)
Other payments*	(54,900)
Closing balance – 31 March 20X9	9,580

*The figure for other payments is for both payments to credit suppliers and drawings, but Jack does not know how much his drawings were in the year.

The loan was taken out on 1 January 20X9 at an interest rate of 6%.

Jack has also provided you with figures for his assets and liabilities at the start and end of the year:

	1 April 20X8 £	31 Mar 20X9 £
Non-current asset cost	10,000	10,000
Inventory	4,100	3,800
Receivables	5,200	4,000
Payables	2,100	2,900
Prepayment of expenses	100	200

The non-current asset originally cost £10,000 on 1 April 20X7 and is being depreciated on the straight line basis over a ten year life.

You now need to prepare the income statement for the year ended 31 March 20X9 and a statement of financial position at that date.

Step 1   Set up the receivables and payables accounts, the expenses account and the cost structure.

Receivables account

£	£

Payables account

£	£

Expenses account

	£		£

Cost structure:

%

Sales
Cost of sales
Gross profit

Step 2 **Work through the task, entering figures as you come across them.**

The cost structure is a profit margin of 25% so the sales must be 100%.

Cost structure:

	%
Sales	100
Cost of sales	75
Gross profit	25

Receivables account

	£		£
Balance b/d	5,200	Bank – receipts	61,200
		Balance c/d	4,000

Expenses account

	£		£
Prepayment b/d	100		
Bank – payments	2,100	Prepayment c/d	200

Payables account

	£		£
		Balance b/d	2,100
Balance c/d	2,900		

Step 3 **Now prepare as much of the trading account as you can, then look at the figures you have prepared to see if they can be slotted into the gaps in the trading account.**

Trading account for the year ended 31 March 20X9

	£	£
Sales		
Less: cost of sales		
Opening inventory	4,100	
Purchases		
Less: closing inventory	(3,800)	
Gross profit		

Now look at the information you have:

- The receivables account has three entries so the missing figure of sales can be determined, and slotted into the trading account:

Receivables account

	£		£
Balance b/d	5,200	Bank – receipts	61,200
Sales	60,000	Balance c/d	4,000
	65,200		65,200

- The payables account has only two entries so no purchases figure can be found yet – but because you know the sales figure, this can be entered into the cost structure to find the cost of sales

Cost structure:

	%	£	
Sales	100	60,000	
Cost of sales	75	45,000	As sales are £60,000
Gross profit	25	15,000	cost must be £60,000
			× 75/100 = £45,000

Take care with this cost of sales figure – it is cost of sales not purchases. However, if you now go to the trading account and apply the opening and closing inventory figures to the cost of sales, the balancing figure is the purchases for the year.

Trading account for the year ended 31 March 20X9

	£	£
Sales		60,000
Less: cost of sales		
Opening inventory	4,100	
Purchases (balancing figure)	44,700	
	48,800	
Less: closing inventory	(3,800)	
		(45,000)
Gross profit		15,000

- The purchases figure of £44,700 has now been found and must be entered as a credit in the payables account:

Payables account

	£		£
		Balance b/d	2,100
Balance c/d	2,900	Purchases	44,700

- The payables account now has three figures so the remaining balance – the payments to payables can be found:

Payables account

	£		£
Payment to payables	43,900	Balance b/d	2,100
Balance c/d	2,900	Purchases	44,700
	46,800		46,800

- Remember from the bank summary that the total for other payments of £54,900 is made up of the payments to payables and the drawings – as we now know the payments to payables the drawings figure can finally be determined:

	£
Total payment	54,900
Less: payment to payables	(43,900)
Drawings	11,000

- The expenses account has three entries and therefore the expenses figure for the income statement can be found as the balancing figure:

Expenses account

	£		£
Prepayment b/d	100	Income statement	2,000
Bank – payments	2,100	Prepayment c/d	200
	2,200		2,200

The opening prepayment must be added in to the bank payment figure as this is part of this year's expense but the closing prepayment must be deducted as this is part of next year's expense.

Step 4   Complete the full income statement

- Do not forget to include the depreciation of the non-current asset as part of the expenses for the year to 31 March 20X9

- We also need to accrue loan interest for the three months from 1 January

Income statement for the year ended 31 March 20X9

	£	£
Sales revenue		60,000
Less: cost of sales		
Opening inventory	4,100	
Purchases	44,700	
	48,800	
Less: closing inventory	(3,800)	
		(45,000)
Gross profit		15,000
Less: expenses		
Expenses	2,000	
Loan interest (£5,000 × 6% × 3/12)	75	
Depreciation (£10,000 × 10%)	1,000	
		(3,075)
Profit for the year		11,925

Step 5   Finally the statement of financial position should be prepared.

For this we will need the opening capital. Using the accounting equation, a list of all the opening assets and liabilities as at 1 April 20X8 is made:

	£
Bank	380
Non-current asset (10,000 – 1,000)*	9,000
Inventory	4,100
Receivables	5,200
Payables	(2,100)
Prepayment	100
Opening capital	16,680

* The asset was purchased on 1 April 20X7 so by 1 April 20X8 – the date for our opening capital – it had been depreciated by one year.

Statement of financial position as at 31 March 20X9

	£	£	£
Non-current asset (10,000 – 2,000)*			8,000
Current assets			
Inventory		3,800	
Receivables		4,000	
Prepayment		200	
Bank		9,580	
		17,580	
Current liabilities			
Payables	2,900		
Accrual – loan interest	75		
		(2,975)	
Net current assets			14,605
			22,605
Non-current liability			
Loan			(5,000)
			17,605
Financed by:			
Opening capital			16,680
Add: profit			11,925
			28,605
Less: drawings			(11,000)
			17,605

*Two years' depreciation has now been charged

Task 7

A business has made sales for a period of £49,000 but the purchases figure is unknown. The sales have been made at a mark-up on cost of 40% and opening and closing inventory were £3,000 and £5,000 respectively.

What were the purchases for the period?

£ [   ]

MISSING INVENTORY FIGURE

A final situation that you may come across in assessments is a missing figure for closing inventory – for example there may have been a fire or flood that destroyed the inventory at the year end before it was counted and valued, or it may have been stolen.

The missing inventory figure must be found as the balancing figure in the trading account – so opening inventory,, sales and purchases must be known and the cost structure used to find the cost of sales – the only figure missing will be the closing inventory.

HOW IT WORKS

Janis Harvey runs a small shop with a mark-up on cost of 30%. Unfortunately her entire inventory at her year end has been stolen before it could be counted and valued. However you have already been able to determine the following figures:

Sales for the year	£52,000
Purchases for the year	£37,000
Opening inventory	£5,000

What was the value of her closing inventory?

We can use the cost structure to determine the total for cost of sales:

	%	£	
Sales	130	52,000	Cost of sales
Cost of sales	100	40,000	$= £52,000 \times \dfrac{100}{130}$
Gross profit	30	12,000	$= £40,000$

The trading account can then be set up:

	£	£
Sales		52,000
Less: cost of sales		
Opening inventory	5,000	
Purchases	37,000	
	42,000	
Less: closing inventory	?	
		40,000
Gross profit		12,000

In order to reach a cost of sales figure of £40,000 the closing inventory must have been valued at £2,000.

Task 8

A business sells its goods at a mark-up on cost of 50%. Sales in the year were £10,500 and purchases were £7,300. The opening inventory was £1,300 but the entire closing inventory has been stolen.

What was the value of the inventory stolen?

£ [   ]

CHAPTER OVERVIEW

- Many small businesses do not keep full accounting records – they have what is known as incomplete records

- There are several techniques that can be used to piece together the information required for an income statement and statement of financial position even if the accounting records are incomplete

- The opening capital balance can be found by applying the accounting equation: assets – liabilities = capital

- The accounting equation can also be expressed as:

  increase in net assets = capital introduced + profit – drawings. This can be used to find a missing figure such as profit or drawings

- The three column cash and bank account can be reconstructed then balanced to find a missing figure such as drawings for the period

- Receivables and payables accounts can also be reconstructed to find missing figures – there are four main entries in these accounts – opening balance, closing balance, cash received/paid, and sales/purchases – if three of the figures are known then the fourth can be found by balancing the account

- Mark-ups and margins for a shop require us to set up the cost structure – this can then be used to find sales if cost of sales is known, or to find cost of sales if sales are known

- All of the techniques covered may be required in an assessment – a clear, logical approach is required together with plenty of practice of incomplete records problems

- The cost structure and the trading account can also be used to find the value of any missing inventory at the end of the accounting period

Keywords

Incomplete records – accounting records which are not a full set of primary records and ledger accounts

Net assets – total of the assets of a business minus the liabilities

Mark-up – the percentage added to cost of goods to arrive at their selling price

Cost structure – the relationship in percentage terms between sales, cost of sales and gross profit

Margin – gross profit expressed as a percentage of sales

TEST YOUR LEARNING

Test 1

A business has made a profit for the year of £17,800. The opening net assets were £58,900 and the closing net assets were £71,400. The owner had paid in an additional £10,000 of capital during the year.

What were the drawings during the year?

£

Test 2

A business had payables on 30 April 20X9 of £4,700 and on 1 May 20X8 of £3,800. During the year payments were made to payables of £56,900 and settlement discounts were received of £1,300.

What were the purchases for the year?

£

Test 3

At 1 April 20X8 a business's bank statement showed a credit balance of £1,020. During the year takings of £48,700 were paid into the bank account and payments for purchases were made of £24,600 and for expenses of £12,500. The closing bank balance was £890.

What were the owner's drawings out of the bank account for the year ending 31 March 20X9?

£

Test 4

A business sells its goods at a mark-up of 45% on cost. The sales for the year were £184,150.

What was the cost of sales for the year?

£

Test 5

A business operates with a margin of 35%. The cost of sales during the year was £130,000.

What were the sales for the year?

£

Test 6

A small business has asked you to help in the preparation of an income statement and statement of financial position for the year ended 31 March 20X9. A summary of the bank statements for the year is given below:

	£
Receipts from receivables	108,500
Payments to payables for purchases	74,400
Payments for expenses	12,600

You are also given the opening and closing figures for the assets and liabilities, however the owner does not know what the closing receivables figure is.

	1 April 20X8 £	31 March 20X9 £
Bank	430	7,200
Inventory	7,600	6,100
Receivables	10,400	not known
Payables	6,200	8,300
Accruals of expenses	800	600

The business also has non-current assets with a carrying amount of £12,600 at 1 April 20X8. It has been decided that £1,600 of depreciation should be charged for the year to 31 March 20X9.

The sales are made at a mark-up of 40%.

Prepare the income statement and statement of financial position for the business for the year ended 31 March 20X9.

Test 7

A business has had all of its closing inventory destroyed by a flood at the end of the year and needs a valuation in order to put in an insurance claim. The information that is known about the business's transactions for the year are:

Sales	£240,000
Purchases	£162,000
Opening inventory	£12,000
Margin	30%

What is the value of the closing inventory that was destroyed?

£

BPP LEARNING MEDIA

chapter 4:
PARTNERSHIPS

chapter coverage 📖

You need to be able to prepare financial statements for two types of business entity: sole traders and partnerships. We looked at sole trader financial statements in Chapter 2, and used sole traders as examples for incomplete records in Chapter 3. In this chapter we will consider the records and accounts of partnerships on the basis that they have complete records.

A partnership is a number of sole traders who are in business together, so the primary records, books of prime entry and ledgers are very similar to those of a sole trader. There are important differences between a sole trader and a partnership however, and in this chapter we will highlight the main ones. The topics that we shall cover are:

- ✍ Definition of a partnership and the partnership agreement

- ✍ Accounting in a partnership for capital, profits and drawings

- ✍ Accounting for partners' salaries and interest on capital using the profit appropriation account

- ✍ Preparing financial statements for a partnership

- ✍ Admission of a new partner

- ✍ Partnership goodwill

- ✍ Retirement of a partner

- ✍ Change in the profit share

PARTNERSHIPS

A partnership is a method of trading which arises where a number of sole traders trade together. A definition of partnership that is in the Partnership Act 1890 is as follows:

'the relation which subsists between persons carrying on a business in common with a view of profit'.

Most partnerships consist of between two and 20 partners, although the large accountancy and legal partnerships have many more partners than this.

Partnership agreement

In a partnership there are a number of owners who pay capital into the business and share the profits of the business. Therefore most partnerships will have a PARTNERSHIP AGREEMENT. This agreement will cover the following common areas:

- How much capital each partner must contribute to the business

- How the profits of the business are shared amongst the partners (the PROFIT SHARE)

- Whether there are any restrictions on partners taking drawings out of the business

- Whether any salaries are to be paid to partners as well as their profit share

- Whether any interest is to be paid to partners on their outstanding capital balance

- Whether partners are to be charged interest on the drawings they take from the partnership

If the partners do not have a partnership agreement then provisions of the Partnership Act 1890 apply. You should be aware of the existence of the Partnership Act 1890 and the circumstances in which the default provisions would be relevant. Recall of the default provisions will not be required in the assessment.

ACCOUNTING IN A PARTNERSHIP

Most of the accounting in a partnership is exactly the same as for a sole trader. Transactions are initially recorded in the books of prime entry and then posted to the general ledger and sales or purchases ledger accounts. There will be the same types of transactions, assets and liabilities in a partnership as for a sole trader.

The difference between a sole trader's accounts and those of a partnership centre around the financing section in the bottom part of the statement of financial position.

For a sole trader, all the capital has been introduced by that sole trader and all the profits and drawings relate to the sole trader. However in a partnership all of the partners contribute capital, they each have a share of the profits and they each take different amounts of drawings. This makes the accounting slightly more complex.

- The capital for each partner is recorded in the partner's CAPITAL ACCOUNT.

- The profits and drawings for each partner are recorded in the partner's CURRENT ACCOUNT.

Capital account

The capital account records the permanent capital that each partner pays into the business:

DEBIT   Bank account

CREDIT   Partner's capital account

This account will only change if there is a permanent increase or decrease in the amount of capital that a partner has in the business. It is not increased by profit shares, nor is it decreased by drawings. These are contained in the current account.

Current account

The current account for each partner is used to record the partner's profit share and the partner's drawings:

Partner's current account

	£		£
Drawings	X	Balance b/d	X
Balance c/d	X	Profit share	X
	X		X
		Balance b/d	X

The balances on each of the partners' capital accounts and current accounts are listed in the bottom part of the partnership statement of financial position.

HOW IT WORKS

Alan, Bill and Chris set up the ABC Partnership on 1 January 20X8. Each partner contributed the following amounts of capital:

Alan	£30,000
Bill	£28,000
Chris	£25,000

In the year ended 31 December 20X8 the income statement shows ABC Partnership made a profit for the year of £60,000, which they have agreed is to be shared equally between the three partners.

The partners took the following drawings in 20X8:

Alan	£12,000
Bill	£15,000
Chris	£16,000

The net assets of the business were £100,000 on 31 December 20X8.

We will write up the partners' capital and current accounts and show them in the statement of financial position at the end of the year.

Capital account – Alan

	£			£
		1 Jan	Bank	30,000

Capital account – Bill

	£			£
		1 Jan	Bank	28,000

Capital account – Chris

	£			£
		1 Jan	Bank	25,000

Current account – Alan

	£		£
31 Dec Drawings	12,000	31 Dec Profit share	20,000
31 Dec Balance c/d	8,000		
	20,000		20,000
		20X9	
		1 Jan Balance b/d	8,000

Current account – Bill

	£		£
31 Dec Drawings	15,000	31 Dec Profit share	20,000
31 Dec Balance c/d	5,000		
	20,000		20,000
		20X9	
		1 Jan Balance b/d	5,000

Current account – Chris

	£		£
31 Dec Drawings	16,000	31 Dec Profit share	20,000
31 Dec Balance c/d	4,000		
	20,000		20,000
		20X9	
		1 Jan Balance b/d	4,000

Here is the bottom part of the statement of financial position:

Statement of financial position extract as at 31 December 20X8:

	£	£
Capital account		
– Alan		30,000
– Bill		28,000
– Chris		25,000
		83,000
Current accounts:		
– Alan	8,000	
– Bill	5,000	
– Chris	4,000	
		17,000
		100,000

This means the statement of financial position balances, as the top part of the statement of financial position, the net assets, total £100,000 at the year end.

Task 1

A partner has paid £24,000 as capital into his partnership. His profit share for the year is £18,000 and he has taken drawings of £13,000 during the year.

What is the balance on the partner's current account at the end of the year?

£

THE PROFIT APPROPRIATION ACCOUNT

In some partnership agreements the profit share arrangements are slightly more complicated, because partners may be:

- Allowed **salaries** to reflect the amount of work they perform within the partnership

- Allowed **interest** on the capital balance that they have within the partnership

- Charged **interest** on any drawings they make if this is more than their opening current account balance

If there are agreements regarding salaries and interest on capital or drawings then the salaries and the interest must be shared out to the partners via the PROFIT APPROPRIATION ACCOUNT **before** the remaining profit is shared out.

HOW IT WORKS

Harry, Bob and Gail are in partnership together with the following partnership agreement:

- Profits are to be shared out in the ratio of 3 : 2 : 1 (this means there are (3+2+1) = 6 equal shares, so Harry gets 3/6 of the available profit, Bob gets 2/6 and Gail gets 1/6)

- Bob has a salary of £10,000 per annum and Gail has a salary of £15,000 per annum

- Interest of 5% is allowed to the partners on their capital balance at the start of each accounting year

At 1 January 20X8 the balances on the partners' capital and current accounts were as follows:

		£
Capital accounts	Harry	50,000
	Bob	30,000
	Gail	20,000
Current accounts	Harry	2,000 (credit)
	Bob	1,000 (debit)
	Gail	1,500 (credit)

During the year ending 31 December 20X8 the partnership made a profit of £120,000. The balance on each partner's drawings account at 31 December 20X8 was as follows:

		£
Drawings accounts	Harry	40,000
	Bob	36,000
	Gail	28,000

The profit for the year of £120,000 is shared out among the partners in the profit appropriation account. This can be shown either as a ledger account or (more usually) in a vertical format. We start with showing it as a ledger account as this helps with the double entry to the partners' current accounts.

Profit appropriation account

£			£
		Balance b/d –profit for the year	120,000

We start the profit appropriation account with the profit for the year as a credit balance. This is the amount due to the partners which is why it is a credit balance – they are 'creditors' of the business. (If there was a loss in a partnership this would be a debit opening balance on the profit appropriation account.)

The profit must now be shared out or 'appropriated' to the partners according to the partnership agreement. All appropriations are:

- Debited to the profit appropriation account and
- Credited to the partners' current accounts.

So we must now set up the partners' current accounts. In this example the current accounts have opening balances on them. These will normally be credit balances as this is the amount of profit due to each partner which the partner has not yet withdrawn in the form of drawings. However in this case Bob has a debit balance on his current account, which means that last year he withdrew more in drawings than was allocated to him in profits. (In the assessment you will be told whether the current account is a credit or debit balance.)

Current account – Harry

	£		£
		Balance b/d	2,000

Current account – Bob

	£		£
Balance b/d	1,000		

Current account – Gail

	£		£
		Balance b/d	1,500

Step 1 **The profit appropriation begins with the allocation of partners' salaries**

The salaries for Bob and Gail are:

- Debited to the profit appropriation account and
- Credited to each partner's current account.

Profit appropriation account

		£		£
Salaries	Bob	10,000	Balance b/d – profit for the year	120,000
	Gail	15,000		

Current account – Bob

	£		£
Balance b/d	1,000	Salary	10,000

Current account – Gail

	£		£
		Balance b/d	1,500
		Salary	15,000

Step 2 **Interest on capital is appropriated to the partners**

The interest to all three partners on their opening capital account balances is appropriated to them:

Harry	£50,000 × 5%	=	£2,500
Bob	£30,000 × 5%	=	£1,500
Gail	£20,000 × 5%	=	£1,000

Profit appropriation account

		£		£
Salaries	Bob	10,000	Balance b/d – profit for the year	120,000
	Gail	15,000		
Interest	Harry	2,500		
on	Bob	1,500		
capital	Gail	1,000		

Current account – Harry

	£		£
		Balance b/d	2,000
		Interest on capital	2,500

Current account – Bob

	£		£
Balance b/d	1,000	Salary	10,000
		Interest on capital	1,500

Current account – Gail

	£		£
		Balance b/d	1,500
		Salary	15,000
		Interest on capital	1,000

Step 3 Share out the remaining profit in the profit share ratio

The remaining profit in this example is shared out to Harry, Bob and Gail in the ratio of 3 : 2 : 1. First we balance the profit appropriation account to determine how much profit remains to be shared out.

Profit appropriation account

		£		£
Salaries	Bob	10,000	Balance b/d – profit for the year	120,000
	Gail	15,000		
Interest	Harry	2,500		
	Bob	1,500		
	Gail	1,000		
Balance c/d		90,000		
		120,000		120,000
			Balance b/d	90,000

We have £90,000 to appropriate to the partners in the profit share ratio:

Harry	£90,000 × 3/6	=	£45,000
Bob	£90,000 × 2/6	=	£30,000
Gail	£90,000 × 1/6	=	£15,000

Profit appropriation account

		£		£
Salaries	Bob	10,000	Balance b/d – profit for the year	120,000
	Gail	15,000		
Interest	Harry	2,500		
on	Bob	1,500		
capital	Gail	1,000		
Balance c/d		90,000		
		120,000		120,000
Profit	Harry	45,000	Balance b/d	90,000
share	Bob	30,000		
	Gail	15,000		
		90,000		90,000

Current account – Harry

	£		£
		Balance b/d	2,000
		Interest on capital	2,500
		Profit share	45,000

Current account – Bob

	£		£
Balance b/d	1,000	Salary	10,000
		Interest on capital	1,500
		Profit share	30,000

Current account – Gail

	£		£
		Balance b/d	1,500
		Salary	15,000
		Interest on capital	1,000
		Profit share	15,000

The profit appropriation account has been cleared, so we know that the full £120,000 profit for the year has been appropriated.

Step 4   The last step is to transfer the balances from the partners' drawings accounts to the debit side of their current accounts, then balance the current accounts so they can be included in the statement of financial position.

Current account – Harry

	£		£
Drawings	40,000	Balance b/d	2,000
		Interest on capital	2,500
Balance c/d	9,500	Profit share	45,000
	49,500		49,500
		Balance b/d	9,500

Current account – Bob

	£		£
Balance b/d	1,000	Salary	10,000
Drawings	36,000	Interest on capital	1,500
Balance c/d	4,500	Profit share	30,000
	41,500		41,500
		Balance b/d	4,500

Current account – Gail

	£		£
Drawings	28,000	Balance b/d	1,500
		Salary	15,000
		Interest on capital	1,000
Balance c/d	4,500	Profit share	15,000
	32,500		32,500
		Balance b/d	4,500

The capital and current account balances will be shown in the bottom part of the statement of financial position as follows:

		£	£
Capital accounts	Harry		50,000
	Bob		30,000
	Gail		20,000
			100,000
Current accounts	Harry	9,500	
	Bob	4,500	
	Gail	4,500	
			18,500
			118,500

Task 2

Petra and Ginger are in partnership together, with the agreement that Ginger receives a salary of £8,000 per annum and that 6% interest is paid on capital balances at the start of the year.

Petra has introduced £40,000 of capital to the business and Ginger £24,000 of capital. At the start of the year Petra had a debit balance of £1,800 on her current account and Ginger had a credit balance on his current account of £500. All profits are to be shared in the ratio of 2 : 1.

Petra took drawings of £38,000 during the year and Ginger withdrew £25,000 from the business. The partnership made a profit of £71,840 during the year.

Write up the profit appropriation account and the partners' current accounts at the year end.

Profit appropriation account

	£		£

Current account – Petra

	£		£

Current account – Ginger

	£		£

Profit appropriation account in vertical format

Usually the profit appropriation account is shown in a vertical format rather than in the ledger account format we saw above. You must remember, though, that it is a ledger account and forms part of the double entry, though it is cleared to zero at each period end.

For Harry, Bob and Gail, the profit appropriation account in vertical format would appear as follows:

		£	£
Profit for the year			120,000
Salaries	Bob	10,000	
	Gail	15,000	
			(25,000)
Interest on capital	Harry	2,500	
	Bob	1,500	
	Gail	1,000	
			(5,000)
Profit available for distribution			90,000
Profit share	Harry	45,000	
	Bob	30,000	
	Gail	15,000	
			90,000

Task 3

Show the profit appropriation account from Task 2 in vertical format.

Profit appropriation account

	£	£
Profit for the year		
Salary		
Interest on capital		
	———	———
Profit available for distribution		═══
Profit share		
	———	———
		═══

Having dealt with the basic accounting for partnerships we will now move on to preparing the financial statements for a partnership from a trial balance.

FROM TRIAL BALANCE TO PARTNERSHIP FINANCIAL STATEMENTS

The financial statements of a partnership can be prepared directly from the trial balance in just the same way as we saw for a sole trader in Chapter 2. Journal entries are required for all year end adjustments and corrections of errors as with a sole trader, but we also need journal entries for the appropriation of the profit between the partners, and for the partners' drawings.

The process is as follows:

- Calculate the profit for the year for the partnership in the income statement ledger account

- Transfer the profit for the year to the profit appropriation account:

  - DEBIT   Income statement ledger account
  - CREDIT   Profit appropriation account

- Next clear the credit balance on the profit appropriation account to the partners' current accounts according to the partnership agreement:

  - DEBIT   Profit appropriation account
  - CREDIT   Partners' current accounts

- Then clear each partner's drawings account by transferring their drawings to the partners' current accounts:

  - DEBIT   Partners' current accounts
  - CREDIT   Partners' drawings accounts

- Finally calculate a balance for each current account to appear in the statement of financial position.

HOW IT WORKS

Tina, Gavin and Fred are in partnership together. For the year ending 30 September 20X8 the income statement ledger account has been prepared and the profit for the year of £120,000 has been transferred to the profit appropriation account. Profits are shared between the three partners in the ratio of 3 : 2 : 1. At 30 September 20X8 the balances on the partners' drawings accounts were:

Tina	£40,000
Gavin	£20,000
Fred	£10,000

We need to prepare the final journal entries required to complete the financial statements of the partnership.

Journal entries

Journal for profit share

	Debit	Credit
Profit and loss appropriation account	£120,000	
Tina – current account (£120,000 × 3/6)		£60,000
Gavin – current account (£120,000 × 2/6)		£40,000
Fred – current account (£120,000 × 1/6)		£20,000

Journal for drawings

		Debit	Credit
Current accounts	Tina	£40,000	
	Gavin	£20,000	
	Fred	£10,000	
Drawings accounts	Tina		£40,000
	Gavin		£20,000
	Fred		£10,000

Task 4

Jane, Mike and Simon are in partnership sharing profits in the ratio of 4 : 3 : 2. During the year ending 30 June 20X8 the partnership made a profit for the year of £180,000 which has been transferred to the profit appropriation account. What is the journal entry required to record the appropriation of profit to the partners?

	Debit £	Credit £

Interest on partners' drawings

We saw earlier that the appropriation of profit is more complicated when the partnership agreement covers salaries for partners and interest on partners' capital. An extra complication arises when the partners are also charged interest on the drawings they make. This may be part of the agreement where the partners wish to discourage each other from taking money out of the business, perhaps because the business is short of cash.

The double entry for interest on drawings is:

DEBIT   Partners' current accounts

CREDIT   Profit appropriation account

It may seem strange that the double entry for interest on drawings increases the balance on the profit appropriation account. In fact it does not increase the net profit made by the business which is available for sharing. Instead, by crediting the interest on drawings to the appropriation account we ensure that the amount available for appropriation in the profit share ratio reflects the fact that some withdraw more than others.

In the assessment you will not have to calculate the interest charge for drawings, but you do need to be able to account for the amounts that are agreed.

HOW IT WORKS

Jenny and Clare are in partnership sharing profits in the ratio of 2 to 1. Clare is allowed a salary of £10,000 per annum and both partners are allowed interest at 4% per annum on their capital balances. They are also charged interest on the drawings that they make during the year.

In the year ending 30 September 20X8 the partnership made a profit for the year of £72,000. An extract from the trial balance at 30 September 20X8 shows the following balances:

		£
Capital	Jenny	30,000
	Clare	20,000
Current account balance at 1 October 20X7 (credit balances)		
	Jenny	2,000
	Clare	3,500
Drawings	Jenny	39,000
	Clare	31,000

The partners have agreed that Jenny will be charged £1,300 interest on her drawings and Clare will be charged £1,100.

First of all we need to determine how the profit of £72,000 is to be appropriated to the partners.

Profit appropriation account

	£		£
Salary: Clare	10,000	Profit for the year	72,000
Interest on capital		Interest on drawings	
Jenny (4% × 30,000)	1,200	Jenny	1,300
Clare (4% × 20,000)	800	Clare	1,100
Balance c/d	62,400		
	74,400		74,400
		Balance b/d	62,400
Profit share			
Jenny (62,400 × 2/3)	41,600		
Clare (62,400 × 1/3)	20,800		
	62,400		62,400

We can see the total amounts to be appropriated to each partner add up to the net profit made by the business:

		£	£
Jenny	Interest on capital	1,200	
	Interest on drawings	(1,300)	
	Profit share	41,600	
			41,500
Clare	Salary	10,000	
	Interest on capital	800	
	Interest on drawings	(1,100)	
	Profit share	20,800	
			30,500
Net profit			72,000

Now the journal entries can be prepared:

	Debit £	Credit £
Profit appropriation account	72,000	
Current account – Jenny		41,500
Current account – Clare		30,500

Being profit share for the year.

Remember the drawings also have to be transferred to the current accounts.

	Debit £	Credit £
Current account – Jenny	39,000	
Current account – Clare	31,000	
Drawings account – Jenny		39,000
Drawings account – Clare		31,000

Finally the current accounts for the partners can be drawn up to give the balances which will appear in the statement of financial position. Don't forget the opening balances on each current account.

Current account – Jenny

	£		£
Drawings	39,000	Balance b/d	2,000
Balance c/d	4,500	Profit share	41,500
	43,500		43,500
		Balance c/d	4,500

Current account – Clare

	£		£
Drawings	31,000	Balance b/d	3,500
Balance c/d	3,000	Profit share	30,500
	34,000		34,000
		Balance b/d	3,000

The figures in the bottom part of the statement of financial position are:

		£	£
Capital accounts	Jenny		30,000
	Clare		20,000
			50,000
Current accounts	Jenny	4,500	
	Clare	3,000	
			7,500
			57,500

Task 5

Frank and Butch are in partnership and the income statement ledger account for the year ending 31 March 20X9 shows they have made a profit for the year of £75,000. The partnership agreement states that Frank should receive a salary of £5,000 per annum, and that interest is paid on capital balances at 5% per annum. Profits are shared equally.

Extracts from the final trial balance are given below:

		£
Capital	– Frank	30,000
	Butch	30,000
Current	– Frank	1,000
	Butch	1,000 (debit balance)
Drawings	– Frank	34,000
	Butch	30,000

Prepare (a) the profit appropriation account and (b) the journal entries required to produce the final balance on the current accounts.

Profit appropriation account

	£	£
Profit for the year		
Salary		
Interest on capital		
	————	————
Profit available for distribution		════
Profit share		
	————	
	════	

Journal entries

	Debit £	Credit £

Combining partners' current accounts

It is often easier when drawing up ledger accounts for partners to use a single ledger account for all the partners' current accounts. For instance, instead of having the two separate accounts for Jenny and Clare:

Current account – Jenny

	£		£
Drawings	39,000	Balance b/d	2,000
Balance c/d	4,500	Profit share	41,500
	43,500		43,500
		Balance b/d	4,500

Current account – Clare

	£		£
Drawings	31,000	Balance b/d	3,500
Balance c/d	3,000	Profit share	30,500
	34,000		34,000
		Balance b/d	3,000

We can combine them as follows:

Current accounts

	Jenny	Clare		Jenny	Clare
		£			£
Drawings	39,000	31,000	Balance b/d	2,000	3,500
Balance c/d	4,500	3,000	Profit share	41,500	30,500
	43,500	34,000		43,500	34,000
			Balance c/d	4,500	3,000

This is a useful technique when it comes to accounting for changes to partnerships, either on admission of a new partner or retirement of an existing one, as we shall see now.

ADMISSION OF A NEW PARTNER

Partners may decide to admit a new partner to the partnership, because the business needs more capital to expand, or more expertise.

Once the terms of the expanded partnership have been agreed, the new partner is required to pay a certain amount of cash into the partnership bank account as his capital. The double entry for this is:

DEBIT   Bank account

CREDIT   New partner's capital account

The agreement between the original partners and the new partner will also cover his profit share in the business, as well as rules on salaries, interest on capital and interest on drawings.

HOW IT WORKS

Kylie and Jake have been in partnership together for a number of years sharing profits in the ratio of 2 to 1. However as the business requires urgent investment in new equipment for expansion they have decided to admit a new partner to the business, Craig. It has been agreed that Craig will join the partnership on 1 April 20X8 and will pay £60,000 into the business bank account as his capital. The profit share for the three partners – Kylie, Jake and Craig – will then be 2 : 2 : 1.

During the year to 31 December 20X8 the partnership made a profit of £120,000.

We will start with the double entry for the capital paid into the partnership by Craig. This is debited to the bank account and credited to a newly opened capital account for Craig.

Capital account – Craig

£		£
	Bank	60,000

At the end of the year to 31 December 20X8 the profits must be shared between the partners. This is done in a two stage calculation:

Step 1   **First the profit for the period up to the admission of Craig is distributed between Kylie and Jake in their old profit share ratio of 2 : 1.**

Profit from 1 January

to 31 March 20X8 (3 months)	=	£120,000 × 3/12
	=	£30,000
Kylie profit share	=	£30,000 × 2/3
	=	£20,000
Jake profit share	=	£30,000 x 1/3
	=	£10,000

Step 2 | The profits for the period from 1 April to 31 December 20X8 must then be distributed between all three partners in the new profit sharing ratio of 2 : 2 : 1.

Profit from 1 April

to 31 December 20X8	=	£120,000 × 9/12
	=	£90,000
Kylie profit share	=	£90,000 × 2/5
	=	£36,000
Jake profit share	=	£90,000 × 2/5
	=	£36,000
Craig profit share	=	£90,000 × 1/5
	=	£18,000

So the total profit for each partner to be credited to their current accounts is:

	Kylie £	Jake £	Craig £
1 Jan to 31 Mar	20,000	10,000	–
1 April to 31 Dec	36,000	36,000	18,000
	56,000	46,000	18,000

An alternative method for appropriating profit over a year in which there has been a change in the partnership is the use of a three-column pro forma profit appropriation account. Steps 1 and 2 above are combined as follows:

Kylie, Jake and Craig – Profit appropriation account for the year ended 31 December 20X8

	1/1/X8–31/3/X8 £	1/4/X8–31/12/X8 £	Total £
Profit available for distribution	30,000	90,000	120,000
Profit share			
Kylie	20,000	36,000	56,000
Jake	10,000	36,000	46,000
Craig		18,000	18,000
	30,000	90,000	120,000

Task 6

A new partner, Howard, is admitted to a partnership and agrees to pay in £25,000 of capital. What is the double entry for the admission of this partner?

Journal entries

	Debit £	Credit £

GOODWILL

The types of non-current asset that we have considered so far in Accounts Preparation I and II have been TANGIBLE NON-CURRENT ASSETS that have a physical form, for example machinery, motor vehicles, computers etc.

There are also INTANGIBLE NON-CURRENT ASSETS which are still held for long term use within the business, but which have no physical form. The most common form of intangible non-current asset is GOODWILL: the extra value in a business that is created by such things as good quality products, excellent after-sales service, good location, loyal workforce etc. Goodwill is a true asset of the business as it means the business makes more sales and earns more profit. However in most cases goodwill does not appear on the statement of financial position because it is difficult to measure it reliably in monetary terms.

However, when there is any form of change in a partnership, the true value of the partnership needs to be recognised. This is done as follows:

- Set up the partnership's goodwill as an asset so that the partnership is correctly valued

- Account for the required change to the partnership (admission or retirement of a partner)

- Remove the goodwill again as it cannot remain in the statement of financial position

HOW IT WORKS

Jane and Pete are in partnership sharing profits 2 : 1. The value of their net assets in the statement of financial position at 30 June 20X8 is £120,000. It is estimated that the goodwill in the business is valued at £24,000. Liam is to be admitted to the partnership on 30 June and the new profit share is to be 3 : 2 : 1. It is agreed that Liam will pay in £24,000 of capital in cash.

With this contribution Liam is buying one sixth of the partnership's net assets, made up as follows:

	£
Statement of financial position net assets (£120,000/6)	20,000
Unrecorded goodwill asset (£24,000/6)	4,000
Capital paid in	24,000

The capital account balances of Jane and Pete at 30 June 20X8 were as follows:

Capital accounts

	Jane £	Pete £			Jane £	Pete £
				30/6 bal b/d	40,000	30,000

Step 1   **The first stage in accounting for the admission of Liam is to set up the goodwill as an asset:**

DEBIT   Goodwill account

CREDIT   Capital accounts with £24,000 goodwill in the **old** profit share ratio of 2 : 1, so 2/3 to Jane (£16,000) and 1/3 to Pete (£8,000):

Goodwill account

	£		£
Capital accounts	24,000		

Capital accounts

	Jane £	Pete £			Jane £	Pete £
				30/6 bal b/d	40,000	30,000
				30/6 Goodwill	16,000	8,000

This is giving Jane and Pete their share of the goodwill that has been built up to date.

Step 2 Introduce Liam and his capital payment of £24,000. We can do this most easily by making the entry in combined capital accounts that we have expanded to three columns to accommodate Liam:

Capital accounts

	Jane £	Pete £	Liam £		Jane £	Pete £	Liam £
				30/6 bal b/d	40,000	30,000	
				30/6 Goodwill	16,000	8,000	
				30/6 Bank			24,000

Step 3 The goodwill must now be removed from the accounting records:

DEBIT Capital accounts with goodwill of £24,000 in the **new** profit sharing ratio of 3 : 2 : 1, so 3/6 to Jane (£12,000), 2/6 to Pete (£8,000) and 1/6 to Liam (£4,000)

CREDIT Goodwill account

Goodwill account

	£		£
Capital accounts	24,000	Capital accounts	24,000

Capital accounts

	Jane £	Pete £	Liam £		Jane £	Pete £	Liam £
30/6 Goodwill	12,000	8,000	4,000	30/6 bal b/d	40,000	30,000	
				30/6 Goodwill	16,000	8,000	
				30/6 Bank			24,000

This has now removed the goodwill from the accounting records.

Step 4 **Finally the capital accounts can be balanced.**

Capital accounts

	Jane £	Pete £	Liam £		Jane £	Pete £	Liam £
30/6 Goodwill	12,000	8,000	4,000	30/6 bal b/d	40,000	30,000	
				30/6 Goodwill	16,000	8,000	
30/6 Bal c/d	44,000	30,000	20,000	30/6 Bank			24,000
	56,000	38,000	24,000		56,000	38,000	24,000
				1/7 Bal b/d	44,000	30,000	20,000

RETIREMENT OF A PARTNER

A further scenario that you may have to deal with is the retirement of a partner. The accounting processes are similar to that for admission of a partner:

- Credit each partner's capital account with their share of the goodwill in the **old** profit share ratio, so the retiring partner can take their share of goodwill as well as their share of the other net assets
- Remove the goodwill from the accounting records using the **new** profit share ratio.

HOW IT WORKS

Jo, Luke and Pat have been in partnership for a number of years sharing profits equally. Jo is about to retire from the partnership and any balances due to her are to be paid to her by the partnership in cash.

At the retirement date the capital and current account balances of the partners were as follows:

		£
Capital accounts	Jo	40,000
	Luke	35,000
	Pat	35,000
Current accounts	Jo	2,000
	Luke	5,000
	Pat	3,000

The goodwill of the partnership was estimated at £30,000. After Jo's retirement, profits are to be shared between Luke and Pat in the ratio of 2 : 1.

Step 1   **Set up the partners' capital accounts and current accounts.**

Capital accounts

Jo £	Luke £	Pat £		Jo £	Luke £	Pat £
			Bal b/d	40,000	35,000	35,000

Current accounts

Jo £	Luke £	Pat £		Jo £	Luke £	Pat £
			Bal b/d	2,000	5,000	3,000

Step 2   Transfer the balance on Jo's current account to her capital account so that all amounts due to Jo are recorded in one account.

Capital accounts

Jo	Luke	Pat		Jo	Luke	Pat
£	£	£		£	£	£
			Bal b/d	40,000	35,000	35,000
			Current a/c	2,000		

Current accounts

	Jo	Luke	Pat		Jo	Luke	Pat
	£	£	£		£	£	£
Capital a/c	2,000			Bal b/d	2,000	5,000	3,000

Step 3   Recognise the goodwill by setting up a goodwill account and crediting each partner with their share of that goodwill in the old profit sharing ratio.

DEBIT   Goodwill account

CREDIT   Partners' capital accounts in **old** profit sharing ratio (£10,000 each since they share equally)

Goodwill

	£		£
Capital accounts	30,000		

Capital accounts

Jo	Luke	Pat		Jo	Luke	Pat
£	£	£		£	£	£
			Bal b/d	40,000	35,000	35,000
			Current a/c	2,000		
			Goodwill	10,000	10,000	10,000

Step 4   **Remove the goodwill from the accounting records.**

DEBIT   Partners' capital accounts in the new profit sharing ratio (£20,000 to Luke and £10,000 to Pat since the new ratio is 2 : 1)

CREDIT   Goodwill account

Goodwill

	£		£
Capital accounts	30,000	Capital accounts	30,000

Capital accounts

	Jo £	Luke £	Pat £		Jo £	Luke £	Pat £
				Bal b/d	40,000	35,000	35,000
				Current a/c	2,000		
Goodwill		20,000	10,000	Goodwill	10,000	10,000	10,000

Step 5 **Calculate the balance on Jo's capital account and pay this amount to her from the bank account**

DEBIT   Capital account with £40,000 + £2,000 + £10,000 = £52,000

CREDIT   Bank

Bank

	£		£
		Capital a/c – Jo	52,000

Capital accounts

	Jo £	Luke £	Pat £		Jo £	Luke £	Pat £
				Bal b/d	40,000	35,000	35,000
				Current a/c	2,000		
Goodwill		20,000	10,000	Goodwill	10,000	10,000	10,000
Bank	52,000						

Step 6 **Finally balance the capital accounts to find the opening capital balances for the two remaining partners.**

Capital accounts

	Jo £	Luke £	Pat £		Jo £	Luke £	Pat £
				Bal b/d	40,000	35,000	35,000
				Current a/c	2,000		
Goodwill		20,000	10,000	Goodwill	10,000	10,000	10,000
Bank	52,000						
Balance c/d		25,000	35,000				
	52,000	45,000	45,000		52,000	45,000	45,000
				Bal b/d		25,000	35,000

Paying off a retiring partner

When a partner retires it is likely that they are owed a significant amount by the partnership, being the capital that they paid into the partnership, the balance on their current account and their share of any goodwill. In many instances the partnership may not have enough money in the bank account to pay off the amount due to the retiring partner. In such circumstances the retiring partner might agree to leave all or part of the amount due to them within the partnership as a loan from the retiring partner.

HOW IT WORKS

Let's return to Jo, Luke and Pat. When Jo retires we have seen that she is owed £52,000 in total by the partnership. Suppose the partners discuss her retirement and agree to pay Jo £12,000 in cash but to keep the remainder as a loan to the partnership from Jo until the partnership has enough cash to pay off the full amount.

In this case the final stages of accounting for the retirement would be slightly different. Having dealt with the goodwill adjustment there will be two remaining accounting entries.

Step 1 **Pay Jo the agreed £12,000.**

DEBIT   Jo's capital account

CREDIT   Bank account

Capital accounts

	Jo £	Luke £	Pat £		Jo £	Luke £	Pat £
				Bal b/d	40,000	35,000	35,000
				Current a/c	2,000		
Goodwill		20,000	10,000	Goodwill	10,000	10,000	10,000
Bank	12,000						

Step 2 **Set up the loan from Jo to the partnership.**

There is a further £40,000 due to Jo which is to remain within the partnership as a loan from Jo. This is therefore transferred from Jo's capital account to a loan account.

DEBIT   Jo's capital account

CREDIT   Loan account – Jo

Capital accounts

	Jo £	Luke £	Pat £		Jo £	Luke £	Pat £
				Bal b/d	40,000	35,000	35,000
				Current a/c	2,000		
Goodwill		20,000	10,000	Goodwill	10,000	10,000	10,000
Bank	12,000						
Loan	40,000						

Loan account – Jo

	£		£
		Capital account	40,000

Step 3   Finally the capital accounts can be balanced as before.

Capital accounts

	Jo £	Luke £	Pat £		Jo £	Luke £	Pat £
				Bal b/d	40,000	35,000	35,000
				Current a/c	2,000		
Goodwill		20,000	10,000	Goodwill	10,000	10,000	10,000
Bank	12,000						
Loan	40,000						
Balance c/d		25,000	35,000				
	52,000	45,000	45,000		52,000	45,000	45,000
				Bal b/d		25,000	35,000

Task 7

Nick, Sue and Trish have been in partnership for a number of years sharing profits equally. At the year end of 31 March 20X9 Sue retired. The partnership between Nick and Trish will continue and profits will be shared in the ratio of 2 : 1.

The capital and current account balances for the partners at the year end of 31 March 20X9 were as follows:

		£
Capital accounts	Nick	50,000
	Sue	40,000
	Trish	30,000
Current accounts	Nick	3,000
	Sue	2,000
	Trish	1,000

Partnership goodwill is estimated to have a value of £15,000. On retirement it has been agreed that Sue will receive £10,000 in cash and the remainder of what is due to her will be retained in the form of a loan to the partnership.

Write up the partners' capital accounts to reflect the retirement of Sue.

Capital accounts

	Nick £	Sue £	Trish £		Nick £	Sue £	Trish £

CHANGE IN PROFIT SHARE RATIO

There is one further important change that might take place within a partnership. During an accounting period the partners might decide to change their agreed profit share. This means there will be two separate profit appropriation calculations – one for the period up to the date of change and one for the period after the date of change. Therefore the total profit made in the year must be split into each of these periods.

HOW IT WORKS

During the year ended 31 December 20X8 the partnership of Phil and Bob made a total profit of £60,000. At the start of the year the profit sharing ratio was 2 : 1 and Phil had a debit balance of £2,000 on his current account while Bob had a credit balance of £1,000. On 31 March 20X8 the partners decided to change the ratio to equal shares of profit and for Phil to receive a salary of £12,000 per annum. The profit has accrued evenly over the year. Phil made drawings of £33,000 during the year and Bob made drawings of £20,000.

Step 1   **In order to appropriate the profit correctly we need firstly to appropriate the profit up to 31 March in accordance with the old profit share ratio of 2 : 1.**

	£
Profit to 31 March (£60,000 × 3/12)	15,000
Appropriation:	
Phil (£15,000 × 2/3)	10,000
Bob (£15,000 × 1/3)	5,000
	15,000

Step 2   Next appropriate the profit for the remainder of the year according to the new agreement. We appropriate the salary for the remainder of the year first, then the balance in the new ratio.

		£
Profit from 1 April to 31 December (£60,000 × 9/12)		45,000
Appropriation:		
Salary	Phil (£12,000 × 9/12)	9,000
Profit share	Phil (£45,000 – £9,000) × 1/2	18,000
	Bob (£45,000 – £9,000) × 1/2	18,000
		45,000

Step 3   Write up the partners' current accounts.

Current accounts

	Phil £	Bob £		Phil £	Bob £
Bal b/d	2,000		Bal b/d		1,000
Drawings	33,000	20,000	Profit to 31 March	10,000	5,000
			Salary	9,000	
Bal c/d	2,000	4,000	Profit to 31 Dec	18,000	18,000
	37,000	24,000		37,000	24,000
			Bal b/d	2,000	4,000

Step 4   Complete the appropriation account for the whole year.

Phil and Bob – Profit appropriation account for the year ended 31 December 20X8

	1/1/X8– 31/3/X8 £	1/4/X8– 31/12/X8 £	Total £
Profit available for distribution	15,000	45,000	60,000
Salary - Phil		9,000	9,000
Profit share			
Phil	10,000	18,000	28,000
Bob	5,000	18,000	23,000
	15,000	45,000	65,000

Task 8

Pat and Ray have been in partnership for a number of years sharing profits in the ratio of 2 : 1. On 31 May 20X8 they decided to change the profit share ratio so that each partner received an equal share of profits. The partnership profit for the year to 31 December 20X8 was £72,000 and this accrued evenly over the year.

The current account balances of the two partners at 1 January 20X8 were a credit balance of £7,400 for Pat and a debit balance of £1,200 for Ray. The partners' drawings for the year were £32,000 for Pat and £19,000 for Ray.

Calculate the profit appropriation for the year and write up the partners' current accounts for the year.

Pat and Ray – Profit appropriation account for the year ended 31 December 20X8

	1/1/X8 – 31/5/X8 £	1/6/X8 – 31/12/X8 £	Total £
Profit available for distribution			
Profit share			

Current accounts

	Pat £	Ray £		Pat £	Ray £
Bal b/d					

CHAPTER OVERVIEW

- A partnership is a number of people in business together trying to make a profit – most partnerships will have a partnership agreement covering the sharing of profits and other financial details

- Most of the accounting for a partnership is the same as that for a sole trader – the difference lies in accounting for the financing of the partnership in the form of capital, profits and drawings

- The partners' capital accounts are used to record the permanent capital that a partner pays into the partnership

- The partners' current accounts are used to record each partner's share of the profits for the year and each partner's drawings during the year

- The profit appropriation account is used to split the profit for the period between the parties. Profit can be appropriated by salary, interest on capital and interest on drawings, then the remaining profit is appropriated in the profit share ratio

- The financial statements are prepared from the final trial balance – journal entries are required to write up the current accounts with profit share and drawings

- If a new partner is admitted to the partnership he or she will pay cash for their share of the partnership assets

- Goodwill must be adjusted for when the new partner is admitted by crediting the partners' capital accounts in the old profit share ratio and debiting the capital accounts in the new profit share ratio

- If a partner retires goodwill must be adjusted by crediting the partners' capital accounts in the old profit share ratio and debiting with the new profit share ratio. The retiring partner's current account balance is also transferred to the capital account. The partnership pays the retiring partner what is due either wholly or partly in cash. Any balance for what is owed remains as a loan from the retiring partner to the partnership

- If the partners change the profit share ratio during the accounting period then the appropriation of profit takes place in two separate calculations. The profit for the period is split into the profit before the change, which is appropriated using the old profit share ratio, and the profit after the change – which is appropriated using the new profit share ratio

Keywords

Partnership agreement – agreement between the partners concerning the sharing out of the profits of the partnership and other financial details

Profit share – how the profits of the business are shared among the partners, normally in a ratio such as 2 : 1

Capital accounts – the accounts that record the permanent capital that each partner pays into the business

Current accounts – the accounts that record the partners' profit share for the year and the partners' drawings for the year

Appropriation – sharing of profit between partners

Profit appropriation account – ledger account used to distribute the profit according to the partnership agreement

Tangible non-current assets – assets held for long term use in the business which have a physical form eg machinery

Intangible non-current assets – assets held for long term use in the business which do not have a physical form eg goodwill

Goodwill – An intangible non-current asset which reflects aspects of the business which add value to the business but which are difficult to value eg well-trained workforce, good customer service

TEST YOUR LEARNING

Test 1

List SIX areas which are likely to be considered when a partnership is drawing up its partnership agreement.

-
-
-
-
-
-

Test 2

Fred and George started in partnership on 1 May 20X8. Fred paid in £32,000 of capital and George £27,000 of capital. During the year ended 30 April 20X9 the business made a profit of £50,000 which is to be split 6 : 4 between Fred and George. Fred's drawings during the year were £20,000 and George's were £16,000.

Write up the capital and current accounts for the two partners for the year and show the balances on these accounts that would appear in the statement of financial position at 30 April 20X9.

Capital account – Fred

Date	Details	£	Date	Details	£

Capital account – George

Date	Details	£	Date	Details	£

Current account – Fred

Date	Details	£	Date	Details	£

Current account – George

Date	Details	£	Date	Details	£

Statement of financial position extract

Test 3

Jake and Lyle were in partnership with the following partnership agreement:

- Jake receives a salary of £10,000 per annum and Lyle receives a salary of £20,000 per annum

- Interest on capital is allowed at 4% per annum

- Profits are to be shared in the ratio of 3 : 2

An extract from the trial balance at 30 September 20X8 shows the following:

		£
Capital accounts at 1/10/X7	Jake	100,000
	Lyle	60,000
Current accounts at 1/10/X7	Jake	5,000
	Lyle	8,000
Drawings	Jake	31,000
	Lyle	34,000

The partnership made a profit for the year of £66,400 in the year ending 30 September 20X8.

Prepare the profit appropriation account and the partners' current accounts, and show the figures that will appear in the statement of financial position for the partners' capital and current accounts.

Profit appropriation account

	£		£

Current account – Jake

Date	Details	£	Date	Details	£

Current account – Lyle

Date	Details	£	Date	Details	£

Statement of financial position extract

	£	£

Test 4

Anna, Bill and Cheryl are in partnership sharing profits in the ratio of 2 : 1 : 1. Bill has a salary of £10,000 and Cheryl has a salary of £5,000 per annum. All partners are allowed interest at 4% on their capital balance.

The final trial balance at 30 June 20X8 is as follows:

Trial balance as at 30 June 20X8

	Debit £	Credit £
Inventory at 1 July 20X7	45,000	
Inventory at 30 June 20X8	50,000	50,000
Depreciation expense	16,000	
Receivables	50,000	
Irrecoverable debts expense	3,500	
Sales		465,000
Non-current assets at cost	80,000	
Accumulated depreciation at 30 June 20X8		58,000
Allowance for doubtful debts at 30 June 20X8		1,000
Expenses	73,000	
Drawings Anna	38,000	
Bill	15,000	
Cheryl	18,000	
Accruals		5,000
Payables		40,000
Bank	2,000	
Current accounts at 1 July 20X7		
Anna		2,500
Bill		5,000
Cheryl		3,000
Purchases	302,000	
Capital accounts		
Anna		30,000
Bill		23,000
Cheryl		10,000
	692,500	692,500

You are required to:

(a) Prepare the income statement of the partnership

(b) Complete the profit appropriation account

(c) Draw up the partners' current accounts

(d) Prepare the statement of financial position as at 30 June 20X8

Test 5

Kate, Hal and Mary have been in partnership for a number of years sharing profits equally, but on 31 December 20X8 Kate decided to retire. During the year ended 31 December 20X8 the partnership made a profit of £75,000.

The partners' capital and current account balances at 1 January 20X8 and their drawings for the year were as follows:

		£
Capital account	Kate	48,000
	Hal	38,000
	Mary	27,000
Current account	Kate	1,200 (credit)
	Hal	800 (debit)
	Mary	2,500 (credit)
Drawings	Kate	20,000
	Hal	23,500
	Mary	24,400

At 31 December 20X8 the goodwill of the partnership was estimated to be £27,000. After Kate's retirement profits will be shared equally between the two remaining partners.

It has been agreed that the partnership will pay Kate £15,000 of the amount due to her in cash and that the remainder should remain as a loan to the partnership.

Write up the capital and current accounts for the partners for the year ending 31 December 20X8.

Capital accounts

Kate £	Hal £	Mary £	Kate £	Hal £	Mary £

Current accounts

	Kate £	Hal £	Mary £		Kate £	Hal £	Mary £

Test 6

Paul and Gill have been in partnership for a number of years sharing profits in the ratio of 3 : 2. On 1 July 20X8 they decided to change the partnership agreement. Gill is to receive a salary of £10,000 per annum and profits are to be distributed in the ratio of 2 : 1. During the year ending 30 September 20X8 the partnership profits totalled £45,000.

At 1 October 20X7 both partners had credit balances of £2,000 on their current accounts. Paul made drawings of £26,400 during the year to 30 September 20X8 and Gill's drawings for the period totalled £18,700.

Write up the partners' current accounts for the year ending 30 September 20X8.

Current accounts

	Paul £	Gill £		Paul £	Gill £

ANSWERS TO CHAPTER TASKS

CHAPTER 1   Introduction to financial statements

1

	Debit	Credit	Asset	Liability	Income	Expense	Capital
	£	£					
Rent	480					✓	
Motor van	7,400		✓				
Payables		1,900		✓			
Gas	210					✓	
Discounts received		50			✓		
Distribution costs	310					✓	
Sales		40,800			✓		
Opening inventory	2,100					✓	
Loan		2,000		✓			
Electricity	330					✓	
Capital		7,980					✓
Telephone	640					✓	
Discounts allowed	60					✓	
Purchases	22,600					✓	
Receivables	3,400		✓				
Wages	9,700					✓	
Drawings	4,000						✓
Office costs	220					✓	
Motor expenses	660					✓	
Bank	620		✓				
	52,730	52,730					

2

	£	£
Sales		136,700
Less: cost of sales		
Opening inventory	11,300	
Purchases	97,500	
	108,800	
Less: closing inventory	(10,600)	
		(98,200)
Gross profit		38,500

3

	Debit	Credit	Income statement	Statement of financial position
	£	£		
Rent	480		✓	
Motor van	7,400			✓
Payables		1,900		✓
Gas	210		✓	
Discounts received		50	✓	
Distribution costs	310		✓	
Sales		40,800	✓	
Opening inventory	2,100		✓	
Loan		2,000		✓
Electricity	330		✓	
Capital		7,980		✓
Telephone	640		✓	
Discounts allowed	60		✓	
Purchases	22,600		✓	
Receivables	3,400			✓
Wages	9,700		✓	
Drawings	4,000			✓
Office costs	220		✓	
Motor expenses	660		✓	
Bank	620			✓
	52,730	52,730		

4   Inventories: IAS 2

Property, plant and equipment: IAS 16

CHAPTER 2 Financial statements for a sole trader

1 £25,700

	£
Opening capital	23,400
Add: profit for the year	14,500
Less: drawings for the year	(12,200)
Closing capital	25,700

2 DEBIT Drawings £400

CREDIT Purchases £400

3 (a) DEBIT Purchases returns

CREDIT Income statement

(b) DEBIT Income statement

CREDIT Insurance

(c) No adjustment required as this is a statement of financial position item.

4 £21,320

	£	£
Sales		45,200
Less: sales returns		(850)
		44,350
Opening inventory	2,500	
Purchases	22,360	
Less: purchase returns	(430)	
	24,430	
Closing inventory	(1,400)	
Cost of sales		(23,030)
Gross profit		21,320

CHAPTER 3   Incomplete records

1   £25,100

	£
Car – valuation	6,000
Computer – valuation	2,500
Inventory	8,900
Receivables	11,200
Payables for purchases	(5,200)
Payables for expenses	(200)
Bank	1,800
Cash in till	100
	25,100

2   £10,200

	£
Opening net assets	31,400
Closing net assets	40,600
Increase in net assets	9,200

Increase in net assets	= capital introduced + profit – drawings
9,200	= 5,000 + 14,400 – drawings
Drawings	= £10,200

3   £38,500

Receivables account

	£		£
Balance b/d	3,300	Receipts	38,700
		Irrecoverable debt written off	300
Credit sales (bal fig)	38,500	Balance c/d	2,800
	41,800		41,800

4   £40,500

Payables account

	£		£
Payments (bal fig)	40,500	Balance b/d	4,100
Balance c/d	3,600	Purchases	40,000
	44,100		44,100

5 £1,500

	%	£
Sales	130	1,950
Cost	100	1,500
Gross profit	30	450

6 £3,333

	%	£
Sales	100	3,333
Cost	60	2,000
Gross profit	40	1,333

7 £37,000

	%	£
Sales	140	49,000
Cost of sales	100	35,000
Gross profit	40	14,000

	£	£
Sales		49,000
Less: cost of sales		
Opening inventory (stock)	3,000	
Purchases (bal fig)	37,000	
	40,000	
Less: closing inventory	(5,000)	
		35,000
Gross profit		14,000

8 £1,600

	%	£
Sales	150	10,500
Cost of sales	100	7,000
Gross profit	50	3,500

	£	£
Sales		10,500
Less: Cost of sales		
Opening inventory	1,300	
Purchases	7,300	
	8,600	
Less: closing inventory	?	
		7,000
Gross profit		3,500

The closing inventory must have been valued at £1,600.

CHAPTER 4   Partnerships

1   £5,000

	£
Profit share	18,000
Less: drawings	(13,000)
Current account balance (credit balance)	5,000

2

Profit appropriation account

	£		£
Salary – Ginger	8,000	Profit for the year	71,840
Interest on capital			
Petra (40,000 × 6%)	2,400		
Ginger (24,000 × 6%)	1,440		
Balance shared 2:1:	40,000		
Petra			
Ginger	20,000		
	71,840		71,840

Current account – Petra

	£		£
Balance b/d	1,800	Interest	2,400
Drawings	38,000	Profit share	40,000
Balance c/d	2,600		
	42,400		42,400
		Balance b/d	2,600

Current account – Ginger

	£		£
Drawings	25,000	Balance b/d	500
		Salary	8,000
		Interest	1,440
Balance c/d	4,940	Profit share	20,000
	29,940		29,940
		Balance b/d	4,940

3 Profit appropriation account

		£	£
Profit for the year			71,840
Salary	Ginger		(8,000)
Interest on capital	Petra	2,400	
	Ginger	1,440	
			(3,840)
Balance to share in profit			60,000
share ratio			
Profit share	Petra (2/3)		40,000
	Ginger (1/3)		20,000
			60,000

4

		Debit £	Credit £
Income statement		180,000	
Current accounts	Jane (£180,000 × 4/9)		80,000
	Mike (£180,000 × 3/9)		60,000
	Simon (£180,000 × 2/9)		40,000

5 Profit appropriation account

		Debit £	Credit £
Profit for the year			75,000
Salary – Frank			(5,000)
Interest on capital	Frank (30,000 × 5%)	1,500	
	Butch (30,000 × 5%)	1,500	
			(3,000)
Profit available for distribution			67,000
Profit share	Frank		33,500
	Butch		33,500
			67,000

Journal entries	Debit	Credit
	£	£
Appropriation account	75,000	
Current account		
Frank (5,000 + 1,500 + 33,500)		40,000
Butch (1,500 + 33,500)		35,000
Being profit share for the year		
Current account – Frank	34,000	
Current account – Butch	30,000	
Drawings account – Frank		34,000
Drawings account – Butch		30,000
Being drawings for the year		

6   DEBIT   Bank account   £25,000

    CREDIT   Howard's capital account   £25,000

7

Capital accounts

	Nick	Sue	Trish		Nick	Sue	Trish
	£	£	£		£	£	£
				Bal b/d	50,000	40,000	30,000
				Current a/c		2,000	
Goodwill	10,000		5,000	Goodwill	5,000	5,000	5,000
Bank		10,000					
Loan		37,000					
Bal c/d	45,000		30,000				
	55,000	47,000	35,000		55,000	47,000	35,000
				Bal b/d	45,000		30,000

8   **Pat and Ray – Profit appropriation account for the year ended 31 December 20X8**

	1/1/X8 – 31/5/X8	1/6/X8 – 31/12/X8	Total
	£	£	£
Profit available for distribution			
£72,000 × 5/12	30,000		
£72,000 × 7/12		42,000	72,000
	30,000	42,000	72,000
Profit share			
Pat 2/3 then 1/2	20,000	21,000	41,000
Ray 1/3 then 1/2	10,000	21,000	31,000
	30,000	42,000	72,000

Current accounts

	Pat £	Ray £		Pat £	Ray £
Bal b/d		1,200	Balance b/d	7,400	
Drawings	32,000	19,000	Profit to 31/5	20,000	10,000
Bal c/d	16,400	10,800	Profit to 31/12	21,000	21,000
	48,400	31,000		48,400	31,000
			Bal b/d	16,400	10,800

Answers to chapter tasks

TEST YOUR LEARNING – ANSWERS

CHAPTER 1   Introduction to financial statements

1

	Debit	Credit	Type of balance	IS or SFP
	£	£		
Sales		41,200	Income	IS
Loan		1,500	Liability	SFP
Wages	7,000		Expense	IS
Non-current assets	7,100		Asset	SFP
Opening inventory	1,800		Expense	IS
Receivables	3,400		Asset	SFP
Discounts received		40	Income	IS
Postage	100		Expense	IS
Bank	300		Asset	SFP
Capital		9,530	Capital	SFP
Rent	500		Expense	IS
Purchases	30,100		Expense	IS
Payables		2,500	Liability	SFP
Discounts allowed	70		Expense	IS
Drawings	3,000		Reduction of capital	SFP
Electricity	800		Expense	IS
Telephone	600		Expense	IS
	54,770	54,770		

2   (a)   The gross profit of a business is the profit from the trading activities.

(b)   The total of the current assets minus the current liabilities is known as net current assets.

(c)   Current liabilities are amounts that are payable within one year.

(d)   Long-term liabilities are amounts payable after more than one year.

3 Materiality concept

4 The four objectives that should be considered when selecting appropriate accounting policies are relevance, reliability, comparability and ease of understanding.

Financial information is relevant if it has the ability to influence the economic decisions of users of that information and is provided in time to influence those decisions. Materiality affects relevance.

Reliable information is a wider concept. In order for information to be reliable it must represent the substance of the transaction or event, it must be free from bias and material error and if there is uncertainty about the information then a degree of caution or prudence must have been applied in making any judgements.

The information in financial statements should be comparable over time and as far as possible between different businesses. Therefore the accounting policies chosen should be applied consistently.

Finally accounting policies should be chosen to ensure ease of understanding by users of the financial statements. Users can be assumed to have a reasonable knowledge of business and economic activities and accounting and a willingness to study the information diligently.

CHAPTER 2   Financial statements for a sole trader

1   £33,452

	£
Opening capital	34,560
Net profit	48,752
	83,312
Less: drawings	(49,860)
Closing capital	33,452

2

		£	£
DEBIT	Drawings	1,500	
CREDIT	Purchases		1,500
OR			
DEBIT	Drawings	2,100	
CREDIT	Sales		2,100

3   Telephone expense = £3,400 + 300 = £3,700
Insurance expense = £1,600 – 200 = £1,400

4   Depreciation charge:

Fixtures and fittings	(12,600 × 20%)	= £2,520
Motor vehicles	(38,500 – 15,500) × 30%	= £6,900

Accumulated depreciation:

Furniture and fittings	3,400 + 2,520	= £5,920
Motor vehicles	15,500 + 6,900	= £22,400

Non-current assets

	Cost	Accumulated depreciation	Carrying amount
	£	£	£
Furniture and fittings	12,600	5,920	6,680
Motor vehicles	38,500	22,400	16,100
			22,780

5 (a) **Initial trial balance**

	Debit £	Credit £
Sales		308,000
Machinery at cost	67,400	
Office equipment at cost	5,600	
Office costs	2,300	
Distribution costs	4,100	
Sales ledger control	38,400	
Telephone expenses	1,800	
Purchases ledger control		32,100
Heat and light	3,100	
Bank overdraft		3,600
Purchases	196,000	
Petty cash	100	
Insurance	4,200	
Accumulated depreciation – machinery		31,200
Accumulated depreciation – office equipment		3,300
Inventory at 1 July 20X7	16,500	
Loan from bank		10,000
Miscellaneous expenses	2,200	
Wages	86,700	
Loan interest	600	
Capital		60,000

Initial trial balance	Debit	Credit
Drawings	20,000	
Allowance for doubtful debts		1,000
Suspense	200	
	449,200	449,200

(b) Journal entries

		Debit £	Credit £
(i)	Heat and light	200	
	Suspense		200
(ii)	Inventory – statement of financial position	18,000	
	Inventory – income statement		18,000
(iii)	Depreciation expense – machinery ((67,400 – 31,200) × 30%)	10,860	
	Accumulated depreciation – machinery		10,860
	Depreciation expense – office equipment (5,600 × 20%)	1,120	
	Accumulated depreciation – office equipment		1,120
(iv)	Loan interest	200	
	Telephone	400	
	Accruals		600
(v)	Prepayments (800 × 3/12)	200	
	Insurance		200
(vi)	Irrecoverable debts expense	1,200	
	Sales ledger control		1,200
	Allowance for doubtful debts adjustment (1,116 – 1,000)	116	
	Allowance for doubtful debts		116

(c) Ledger accounts

(i)

Heat and light

		£			£
30 June	Balance b/d	3,100			
30 June	Journal	200	30 June	Balance c/d	3,300
		3,300			3,300
30 June	Balance b/d	3,300			

Suspense account

		£			£
30 June	Balance b/d	200	30 June	Journal	200

(ii)

Inventory – statement of financial position

		£		£
30 June	Journal	18,000		

Inventory – income statement

		£				£
			30 June	Journal		18,000

(iii)

Depreciation expense – machinery

		£		£
30 June	Journal	10,860		

Accumulated depreciation – machinery

		£			£
			30 June	Balance b/d	31,200
30 June	Balance c/d	42,060	30 June	Journal	10,860
		42,060			42,060
			30 June	Balance b/d	42,060

Depreciation expense – office equipment

		£		£
30 June	Journal	1,120		

Accumulated depreciation – office equipment

		£			£
			30 June	Balance b/d	3,300
30 June	Balance c/d	4,420	30 June	Journal	1,120
		4,420			4,420
			30 June	Balance b/d	4,420

(iv)

Loan interest

		£			£
30 June	Balance b/d	600			
30 June	Journal	200	30 June	Balance c/d	800
		800			800
30 June	Balance b/d	800			

Telephone

		£			£
30 June	Balance b/d	1,800			
30 June	Journal	400	30 June	Balance c/d	2,200
		2,200			2,200
30 June	Balance b/d	2,200			

Accruals

		£				£
			30 June	Journal		600

(v)

Prepayments

		£			£
30 June	Balance b/d	200			

Insurance

		£			£
30 June	Balance b/d	4,200	30 June	Journal	200
			30 June	Balance c/d	4,000
		4,200			4,200
30 June	Balance b/d	4,000			

(vi)

Irrecoverable debts expense

		£			£
30 June	Journal	1,200			

Sales ledger control

		£			£
30 June	Balance c/d	38,400	30 June	Journal	1,200
			30 June	Balance c/d	37,200
		38,400			38,400
30 June	Balance b/d	37,200			

Allowance for doubtful debts adjustment

		£			£
30 June	Journal	116			

Allowance for doubtful debts

		£			£
			30 June	balance b/d	1,000
30 June	Balance c/d	1,116	30 June	Journal	116
		1,116			1,116
			30 June	Balance b/d	1,116

(d) Income statement for the year ending 30 June 20X8

	£	£
Sales revenue		308,000
Cost of sales		
Opening inventory	16,500	
Purchases	196,000	
	212,500	
Less: closing inventory	(18,000)	
		(194,500)
Gross profit		113,500
Less: expenses		
Office costs	2,300	
Distribution costs	4,100	
Telephone	2,200	
Heat and light	3,300	
Insurance	4,000	
Miscellaneous expenses	2,200	
Wages	86,700	
Loan interest	800	
Depreciation – machinery	10,860	

	£	£
Depreciation – office equipment	1,120	
Allowance for doubtful debts adjustment	116	
Irrecoverable debts	1,200	
		118,896
Loss for the year		(5,396)

Statement of financial position as at 30 June 20X8

	Cost	Accumulated depreciation	Carrying value
	£	£	£
Non-current assets			
Machinery	67,400	42,060	25,340
Office equipment	5,600	4,420	1,180
	73,000	46,480	26,520
Current assets			
Inventory		18,000	
Receivables	37,200		
Less: allowance	(1,116)		
		36,084	
Prepayments		200	
Petty cash		100	
		54,384	
Current liabilities			
Payables	32,100		
Bank overdraft	3,600		
Accruals	600		
		36,300	
Net current assets			18,084
			44,604
Long term loan			(10,000)
			34,604
Capital			60,000
Loss for the year			(5,396)
			54,604
Less: drawings			(20,000)
			34,604

CHAPTER 3   Incomplete records

1   £15,300

		£
Opening net assets		58,900
Closing net assets		71,400
Increase in net assets		12,500

Increase in net assets	=	capital introduced + profit – drawings
£12,500	=	£10,000 + 17,800 – drawings
Drawings	=	£15,300

2   Purchases = £59,100

Payables account

	£		£
Payments	56,900	Balance b/d	3,800
Discounts	1,300		
Balance c/d	4,700	Purchases (bal fig)	59,100
	62,900		62,900

3   Drawings = £11,730

Bank account

	£		£
Balance b/d	1,020	Purchases	24,600
Receipts	48,700	Expenses	12,500
		Drawings (bal fig)	11,730
		Balance c/d	890
	49,720		49,720

4   Cost of sales = £127,000

	%	£
Sales	145	184,150
Cost of sales	100	127,000
Gross profit	45	57,150

5   Sales = £200,000

	%	£
Sales	100	200,000
Cost of sales	65	130,000
Gross profit	35	70,000

6

Receivables account

	£		£
Balance b/d	10,400	Receipts	108,500

Payables account

	£		£
Payments	74,400	Balance b/d	6,200
Balance c/d	8,300	Purchases (bal fig)	76,500
	82,700		82,700

Cost structure:

	%
Sales	140
Cost of sales	100
Gross profit	40

If purchases are £76,500 then the cost of sales is:

	£
Opening inventory	7,600
Purchases	76,500
	84,100
Less: closing inventory	(6,100)
	78,000

Using the cost structure the sales figure can be determined:

Cost structure:

	%	£
Sales	140	109,200
Cost of sales	100	78,000
Gross profit	40	31,200

The sales figure can then be entered into the receivables account and the closing balance found.

Receivables account

	£		£
Balance b/d	10,400	Receipts	108,500
Sales	109,200	Balance c/d	11,100
	119,600		119,600

The income statement can now be prepared:

Income statement for the year ended 31 March 20X9

	£	£
Sales revenue		109,200
Less: cost of sales		
Opening inventory	7,600	
Purchases	76,500	
	84,100	
Less: closing inventory	(6,100)	
		(78,000)
Gross profit		31,200
Less: expenses		
Expenses (12,600 – 800 + 600)	12,400	
Depreciation	1,600	
		(14,000)
Profit for the year		17,200

In order to draw up the statement of financial position we need the opening capital and the drawings figures.

Net assets at 1 April 20X8

	£
Bank	430
Inventory	7,600
Receivables	10,400
Payables	(6,200)
Accrual	(800)
Non-current assets	12,600
Opening capital	24,030

The drawings can be found as the balancing figure in the bank account:

Bank account

	£		£
Balance b/d	430	Payables	74,400
Receipts from receivables	108,500	Expenses	12,600
		Drawings (bal fig)	14,730
		Balance c/d	7,200
	108,930		108,930

Statement of financial position as at 31 March 20X9

	£	£	£
Non-current assets (12,600 – 1,600)			11,000
Current assets:			
Inventory		6,100	
Receivables		11,100	
Bank		7,200	
		24,400	
Current liabilities:			
Payables	8,300		
Accruals	600		
		(8,900)	
Net current assets			15,500
			26,500
Financed by:			
Opening capital			24,030
Add: profit for the year			17,200
			41,230
Less: drawings			(14,730)
			26,500

7   £6,000

Cost structure:

	%	£
Sales	100	240,000
Cost of sales	70	168,000
Gross profit	30	72,000

	£	£
Sales		240,000
Less: cost of sales		
Opening inventory	12,000	
Purchases	162,000	
	174,000	
Less: closing inventory	?	
		168,000
Gross profit		72,000

Therefore the closing inventory value must be £6,000

CHAPTER 4   Partnerships

1
- How much capital each partner should introduce
- Whether there should be any restrictions on partners taking drawings out of the business
- Whether interest on capital should be allowed
- Whether interest on drawings should be charged
- Whether partners should be allowed any salaries
- How the profit should be shared between the partners

2

Capital account – Fred

Date	Details	£	Date	Details	£
			1 May 20X8	Bank	32,000

Capital account – George

Date	Details	£	Date	Details	£
			1 May 20X8	Bank	27,000

Current account – Fred

Date	Details	£	Date	Details	£
30 Apr 20X9	Drawings	20,000	30 Apr 20X9	Profit share	30,000
30 Apr 20X9	Balance c/d	10,000			
		30,000			30,000
			1 May 20X9	Balance b/d	10,000

Current account – George

Date	Details	£	Date	Details	£
30 Apr 20X9	Drawings	16,000	30 Apr 20X9	Profit share	20,000
30 Apr 20X9	Balance c/d	4,000			
		20,000			20,000
			1 May 20X9	Balance b/d	4,000

Statement of financial position extract

	£	£
Capital accounts:		
Fred		32,000
George		27,000
		59,000
Current accounts:		
Fred	10,000	
George	4,000	
		14,000
		73,000

3

Profit appropriation account

	£		£
Salaries Jake	10,000	Profit for the year	66,400
Lyle	20,000		
Interest			
Jake (100,000 × 4%)	4,000		
Lyle (60,000 × 4%)	2,400		
Balance c/d	30,000		
	66,400		66,400
		Balance b/d	30,000
Profit share			
Jake (30,000 × 3/5)	18,000		
Lyle (30,000 × 2/5)	12,000		
	30,000		30,000

Current account – Jake

	£		£
Drawings	31,000	Balance b/d	5,000
		Salary	10,000
		Interest	4,000
Balance c/d	6,000	Profit share	18,000
	37,000		37,000
		Balance b/d	6,000

Current account – Lyle

	£		£
Drawings	34,000	Balance b/d	8,000
		Salary	20,000
		Interest	2,400
Balance c/d	8,400	Profit share	12,000
	42,400		42,400
		Balance b/d	8,400

Statement of financial position extract

		£	£
Capital accounts	Jake	100,000	
	Lyle	60,000	
			160,000
Current accounts	Jake	6,000	
	Lyle	8,400	
			14,400
			174,400

4 **(a) Income statement for the year ending 30 June 20X8**

	£	£
Sales revenue		465,000
Less: cost of sales		
opening inventory	45,000	
Purchases	302,000	
	347,000	
Less: closing inventory	(50,000)	
		(297,000)
Gross profit		168,000
Less: expenses	73,000	
Depreciation	16,000	
Irrecoverable debts	3,500	
		92,500
Profit for the year		75,500

(b) Profit appropriation account

		£	£
Profit for the year			75,500
Salaries Bill		10,000	
Cheryl		5,000	
			(15,000)
Interest on capital			
Anna	30,000 × 4%	1,200	
Bill	23,000 × 4%	920	
Cheryl	10,000 × 4%	400	
			(2,520)
Profit available for distribution			57,980
Profit share			
Anna	57,980 × 2/4	28,990	
Bill	57,980 × 1/4	14,495	
Cheryl	10,000 × 4%	14,495	
			57,980

(c) **Current accounts**

Current account – Anna

	£		£
Drawings	38,000	Balance b/d	2,500
		Interest	1,200
		Profit share	28,990
		Balance c/d	5,310
	38,000		38,000
Balance b/d	5,310		

Current account – Bill

	£		£
Drawings	15,000	Balance b/d	5,000
		Salary	10,000
		Interest	920
Balance c/d	15,415	Profit share	14,495
	30,415		30,415
		Balance b/d	15,415

Current account – Cheryl

	£		£
Drawings	18,000	Balance b/d	3,000
		Salary	5,000
		Interest	400
Balance c/d	4,895	Profit share	14,495
	22,895		22,895
		Balance b/d	4,895

(d) **Statement of financial position as at 30 June 20X8**

	Cost	Accumulated depreciation	Carrying amount
	£	£	£
Non-current assets	80,000	58,000	22,000
Current assets			
Inventory		50,000	
Receivables	50,000		
Less: allowance	(1,000)		
		49,000	
Bank		2,000	
		101,000	

	Cost £	Accumulated depreciation £	Carrying amount £
Current liabilities			
Payables	40,000		
Accrual	5,000		
		(45,000)	
Net current assets			56,000
			78,000
Capital accounts			30,000
Anna			23,000
Bill			10,000
Cheryl			63,000
		(5,310)	
Current accounts		15,415	
Anna			
Bill		4,895	
Cheryl			15,000
			78,000

5

Capital accounts

	Kate £	Hal £	Mary £		Kate £	Hal £	Mary £
				Bal b/d	48,000	38,000	27,000
				Current a/c	6,200		
Goodwill		13,500	13,500	Goodwill	9,000	9,000	9,000
Bank	15,000						
Loan	48,200						
Bal c/d		33,500	22,500				
	63,200	47,000	36,000		63,200	47,000	36,000

Current accounts

	Kate £	Hal £	Mary £		Kate £	Hal £	Mary £
Bal b/d		800		Bal b/d	1,200		2,500
Drawings	20,000	23,500	24,400	Profit	25,000	25,000	25,000
Capital a/c	6,200						
Bal c/d		700	3,100				
	26,200	25,000	27,500		26,200	25,000	27,500

6

Current accounts

	Paul	Gill		Paul	Gill
	£	£		£	£
Drawings	26,400	18,700	Bal b/d	2,000	2,000
			Profit	20,250	13,500
			Salary		2,500
Bal c/d	1,683	2,217	Profit	5,833	2,917
	28,083	20,917		28,083	20,917

Workings

Profit appropriation

	£
1 Oct to 30 June (£45,000 × 9/12)	33,750
Paul (£33,750 × 3/5)	20,250
Gill (£33,750 × 2/5)	13,500
	33,750
1 July to 30 Sept (£45,000 × 3/12)	11,250
Paul ((£11,250 – 2,500) × 2/3)	5,833
Gill salary	2,500
Gill profit ((£11,250 – 2,500) × 1/3)	2,917
	11,250

OR

	1/10 – 30/6	1/7/ – 30/9	Total
	£	£	£
Profit for distribution	33,750	11,250	45,000
Paul: profit share	20,250	5,833	26,083
Gill: salary		2,500	2,500
Gill: profit share	13,500	2,917	16,417
	33,750	11,250	45,000

INDEX

REVIEW FORM

How have you used this Text?
(Tick one box only)

☐ Home study

☐ On a course_____

☐ Other _____

Why did you decide to purchase this Text? *(Tick one box only)*

☐ Have used BPP Texts in the past

☐ Recommendation by friend/colleague

☐ Recommendation by a college lecturer

☐ Saw advertising

☐ Other _____

During the past six months do you recall seeing/receiving either of the following?
(Tick as many boxes as are relevant)

☐ Our advertisement in Accounting Technician

☐ Our Publishing Catalogue

Which (if any) aspects of our advertising do you think are useful?
(Tick as many boxes as are relevant)

☐ Prices and publication dates of new editions

☐ Information on Text content

☐ Details of our free online offering

☐ None of the above

Your ratings, comments and suggestions would be appreciated on the following areas of this Text.

	Very useful	Useful	Not useful
Introductory section	☐	☐	☐
Quality of explanations	☐	☐	☐
How it works	☐	☐	☐
Chapter tasks	☐	☐	☐
Chapter Overviews	☐	☐	☐
Test your learning	☐	☐	☐
Index	☐	☐	☐

	Excellent	Good	Adequate	Poor
Overall opinion of this Text	☐	☐	☐	☐

Do you intend to continue using BPP Products?   ☐ Yes   ☐ No

Please note any further comments and suggestions/errors on the reverse of this page. The author of this edition can be e-mailed at: paulsutcliffe@bpp.com

Please return to: Paul Sutcliffe, Senior Publishing Manager, BPP Learning Media Ltd, FREEPOST, London, W12 8BR.

REVIEW FORM (continued)

TELL US WHAT YOU THINK

Please note any further comments and suggestions/errors below.

Notes

Notes

Notes

Notes

Notes

Notes